IMPORTANT BILLING AND CREDIT REQUIREMENTS

The following credit *must* appear on the title page of all programs and on all posters, ads and other promotional material issued in connection with productions of the play whenever the producer's name appears, and *must* appear in the credits of any recorded broadcast audio-visual production in any medium:

> The American Premiere of NOT ABOUT HEROES was presented by the Williamstown Theatre Festival, Nikos Psacharapoulos, Artistic Director.

If any subsequent production of the play shall have the same director and/or two of the same actors as the Williamstown Theatre Festival production, Williamstown Theatre Festival *must* receive billing and credit below the title on lines by itself immediately after the Author's name and/or wherever and whenever the producer's name appears, of the same size, type and prominence afforded to the producer. The language of the credit *must* be as follows:

> Produced by arrangement with the Williamstown Theatre Festival, Nikos Psacharapoulos, Artistic Director.

A NOTE ON THE PLAY

When Wilfred Owen was sent to Craiglockhart War Hospital for Nervous Disorders in June, 1917, he was suffering from shell-shock after four months in the trenches in France. It seems that his Commanding Officer equated shell-shock with cowardice. Owen was completely unknown. He aspired to be a poet, but had achieved nothing of note. He was killed in November, 1918. He had won the Military Cross a month before his death. He is now widely recognised as the greatest of the many British poets of the First World War. *Not About Heroes* is concerned with this transformation and how it might have happened.

The crucial event was the meeting with Siegfried Sassoon. He was a well known, acclaimed poet and a soldier of remarkable courage, who had achieved notoriety by publishing a protest against the "evil and unjust" conduct of the war. He was sent to Craiglockhart Hospital at the end of July, 1917, possibly to undermine the strength of his protest by questioning his sanity. Wilfred Owen nervously introduced himself about two weeks later. They had little in common but a warm and loving friendship developed. Owen described it fully in his letters, but Sassoon waited until 27 years after Owen's death before he expressed the strength of his feelings in *Siegfried's Journey,* and even more in the maunscript notes for that book. The friendship seems to have been the key which unlocked Owen's genius as a poet. I also believe, from the tone of Owen's subsequent letters, that it liberated the man.

A NOTE ON THE PLAY
(continued)

This story of their friendship is told almost entirely in my own words. The play is neither a compilation nor a documentary. While I have not intentionally falsified any of the known facts, the Letters and Memoirs leave considerable gaps which I have bridged with scenes based on ideas suggested by the available sources. I have used phrases from Owen's letters (and frequently linked sections from several of them to form a single letter) but there are no surviving letters from Sassoon to Owen. The Sassoon letters in the play reflect his feelings and opinions at the time, but they are not his words.

Sassoon's *Diaries for 1915-1918* were published after the play was written, but I have not found it necessary to revise the play in the light of what they reveal. On the contrary, they have sometimes confirmed conclusions I had drawn from other evidence (e.g. the death of David Thomas in March 1916). But the diaries covering the period at Craiglockhart and the last meeting seem, unfortunately, to have been lost.

Sassoon decided on several occasions that he would write a memoir of Owen, but clearly found the prospect too painful. I believe that the inevitable guilt of the survivor was something he had to live with throughout his long life. He was a deeply reticent as well as a turbulently emotional man, and I hope I have respected his reticence. My motive was to try to understand how a relationship that remains at heart mysterious, could leave such an indelible mark on the literature of their war — and so on our understanding of war itself. My best hope is that *Not About Heroes* might refresh the memory of who these men were and what it was they had to tell us.

Stephen MacDonald
31st March 1986.

THE CHARACTERS

SIEGFRIED SASSOON — *Born in Kent, 8th September, 1886; died, Wiltshire, 1st September, 1967, a week before his 81st birthday.*

WILFRED OWEN — *Born in Oswestry, Shropshire, 18th March, 1893; killed in action on the Oise-Sambre Canal, 4th November, 1918, a week before the Armistice and the end of the First World War.*

THE ACTION

From a room in Sassoon's country house in Wiltshire, late at night on 3rd November, 1932, Sassoon re-lives incidents which happened between August 1917 and November 1918. In sequence, they take place in:

> a quiet corner of the Conservative Club in Edinburgh, (3rd November, 1917);
> two rooms in the Craiglockhart War Hospital for Nervous Disorders, Edinburgh (August-October, 1917);
> the countryside near Milnathort, Scotland, (October, 1917);
> Owen's room in Scarborough, Yorkshire, (January, 1918);
> Sassoon's room in the American Red Cross Hospital, London, and in the hospital garden, (August, 1918);
> a dugout in Flanders, (October-November, 1918).

A NOTE ON THE SETTING

This revision of the play has been made in the light of the production by *Michael Simpson* at the *National Theatre,* which opened on 13th February, 1986. Stage Directions are included in an endeavour to clarify both the intention and the action. They generally follow the line of that production, in the setting designed by *Alison Chitty.*

A stage-cloth covered the down-stage floor, and the upstage end was lifted to form a sky-cloth. The pattern of a Persian carpet painted on the floor defined the area of Sassoon's study. All the exterior action took place upstage, where the cloth was painted in a neutral colour.

As in the first production, the interior was arranged to represent a room in Sassoon's house in Wiltshire, and all the furnishings used in the action (two armchairs, two writing tables, with chairs, a hatstand, an oak chest, etc.) belonged to the room. Milnathort, the Hospital garden and some of Owen's appearances were placed in the area upstage of the room, and lighting effectively shifted the location. For Owen's return to France and the sequences in the dug-out, lighting again created a vivid impression of battle without resorting to reproductions of actual war-pictures. The objective was to allow time and place to move as Sassoon remembered them, and not to be held up by scene or furniture changes.

HISTORY OF THE PLAY

First produced by the Dundee Theatre Company at the Edinburgh Festival in August, 1982. It won the *Scotsman's* Fringe First Award. Sassoon was played by Stephen Mac-Donald, Owen by David Learner, and the play was directed by Eric Standidge.

Afterwards, it was performed at the King's Head in London in March and April 1983, and it was adapted for Yorkshire Television and BBC Radio Four. On these occasions, Owen was played by James Telfer.

In 1986, to mark the centenary of the birth of Siegfried Sassoon, a new production of the revised play was presented at the National Theatre in London. Sassoon was again played by Stephen MacDonald, and Owen by Simon Dutton. The director was Michael Simpson and the designer, Alison Chitty.

* * * * * * *

The Williamstown Theatre Festival production of August, 1985, transferred to the Lucille Lortel Theater, New York, in October 1985. Sassoon was played by Edward Herrmann, Owen by Dylan Baker and the director was Dianne Wiest. Both of the actors won OBIE Awards for their performances in the play.

NOT ABOUT HEROES

ACT ONE

Darkness.
Music may be heard, mysterious and remote.
Light comes up on SASSON's face. Everything else remains in darkness.

SASSOON. Wilfred ... ? Was it my fault? *(Music continues.)* I'd no idea you'd alrteady decided. If I'd known... *(He stops. Tries to explain.)* I wanted you to ... I wanted you ... On that last night, before you... *(He starts to remember.)* Before you go...

(Lights reveal him sitting in a leather armchair. A second armchair is on the other side of a small table, on which there is an almost empty bottle of Burgundy and two glasses. Music fades out.

OWEN enters, in uniform. He carries his cap, gloves and cane, and also a small shoulder pack. He seems to be about to leave.

SASSOON is holding a copy of Aylmer Strong's 'A Human Voice', a thin book bound in dark blue cloth. He offers it, his tone sounding almost casual.)

SASSOON. Oh, yes. Before you go — I want you to have this.

OWEN. Another farewell present?

SASSOON. What do you mean, another?

OWEN. You've already given me one book. "Under Fire". Don't you remember?

SASSOON. That was an attempt to stop you from going. This is to make you laugh as you go. *(OWEN'S smile fades. They have argued this before.)*

OWEN. You make it sound as if it was my decision.

SASSOON. Well, isn't it? I asked Doctor Rivers. You could have stayed on at the hospital.

OWEN. *(trying to avoid what might become a quarrel)* I wanted to stay — with you ... And the rest.

SASSOON. *(exploding)* Then why are you being so bloody pig-headed?!!

OWEN. *(looking around)* Don't shout — the waiters can hear you. *(OWEN sits in the other chair.)* And I must say, you're a fine one to call *me* pig-headed.

SASSOON. *(more quietly)* You still have the dreams. I've heard you.

OWEN. I can't do anything about that.

SASSOON. You can tell the doctors! You should never have been passed fit.

OWEN. I'm only passed fit for light duties. But look — my hands have stopped shaking. The stammer has almost gone. I can't hide in Craiglockhart for the rest of the war, can I?

SASSOON. *(relenting)* No — we can't hide. Or be hidden, either. Oh ... I'm sorry. *(The anger has gone as suddenly as it came. OWEN looks at him with affection, then asks, smiling.)*

OWEN. Is there something special about the fourth of November?

SASSOON. What do you mean?

OWEN. I've never heard you apologise before.

SASSOON. Yes, well ... Don't let it go to your head. *(looks at his watch)* Anyway, there's still half an hour left of the *third* of November.

OWEN. Half an hour ... Come on, what's this book you were going to give me?

SASSOON. Oh, yes. I hope it inspires you. Or acts as an awful warning.

OWEN. *(reading from the fly leaf)* "From Siegfried Sassoon. Edinburgh 1917.
When Captain Cook first sniff'd the wattle
And love Columbus'd Aristotle...."
What does that mean?

SASSOON. Don't ask me. Ask the author. It's a quotation from the book.

OWEN. Aylmer Strong ... Never heard of him.

SASSOON. Haven't you? He sent it to me himself.

OWEN. You know him, then?

SASSOON. Certainly not. Even if I did, do you think I'd admit to it?

OWEN. Then why should he send it to you?

SASSOON. Look at the Foreword.

OWEN. *(reading)* "The proceeds of this book are intended to swell the funds of hospitals established for the care of critical nerve-cases from the Fronts..." Oh, I see.

SASSOON. Yes. And as if shell shock weren't enough, he piles on poetic palsy. Here — *(taking the book from OWEN)* there's another one you might enjoy ... Yes, here it is. "What cassock'd misanthrope,
Hawking Peace Canticles for glory gains

Jars, in mid ecstasy, th'epopt of hate."
Remarkable. He crams in more consonants than even you do. *(OWEN is expressionless. Their game is to see who will be the first to laugh.)*

OWEN. The *what* of hate?

SASSOON. The'epopt, of course.

OWEN. Of course ... What's a popt?

SASSOON. Not *a* popt, *e*popt. *The* epopt. The'*e*popt!

OWEN. I see ... What's an *e*popt?

SASSOON. Not entirely sure. Sounds like something rather worrying you buy in a chemist's shop. *(Then the laughter explodes. OWEN is the one with the loudest laugh and SASSOON finds it infectious. Eventually:)*

SASSOON. Ssshhh...! The waiters...!

OWEN. Sorry ... This is priceless. I'll treasure it.

SASSOON. *(an embarrassed mumble)* It's nothing ... All rubbish.

OWEN. *(regarding him, smiling)* I never know how to thank you.

SASSOON. Don't be silly. No need for thanks.

OWEN. That's exactly *why* I never know. You're so grand.

SASSOON. No need for ingratitude, either.

OWEN. *And* stuck up.

SASSOON. That is absolute rubbish...!

OWEN. And very English, and much too kind.

SASSOON. Mmmm ... *(OWEN looks at his watch.)*

OWEN. Well...

SASSOON. Well?

OWEN. I think I should go for my train.

SASSOON. Ah. Waverley?

OWEN. At midnight.

SASSOON. In that case—

OWEN. I should.

SASSOON. It's home to Shrewsbury, first?

OWEN. Then London, then report to Scarborough in three weeks' time.

SASSOON. Scarborough...

OWEN. *Not* the *Somme...!*

SASSOON. Not *yet! (relenting)* No, not yet. Oh ... *(He seems to gulp down air.)* I shall be ... When you've gone ... so ...

OWEN. *(coming to his rescue)* I've been very proud, you know. Proud of your friendship. Boasting about it to everybody I've met since August — that first day when I knocked at your door.

SASSOON. Timid as a harvest mouse. You *looked* rather like a harvest mouse, too. Eyes wide with awe—

OWEN. —of the Great Hero, the Great Poet.

SASSOON. Until you got to know me better.

OWEN. And then it was more than pride. *(A moment, then SASSOON takes a brown sealed envelope from his pocket.)*

SASSOON. I nearly forgot. You'll need this.

OWEN. Not another present...?

SASSOON. Not really. Travelling instructions. Could be of use. Hope so. So ... It's been ... good. *(SASSOON offers his hand. OWEN does not take it.)*

OWEN. It's been ... *(OWEN is about to embrace him, but SASSOON stops him, and when he speaks he sounds angry.)*

SASSOON. You must take great care of yourself — for me — for all of us.

OWEN. *(smiling)* Is that an order?

SASSOON. A strict order.

OWEN. Then I will. For you. *(Suddenly, they hug each other. There is probably as much fear as love. They let go. SASSOON looks around.)*

SASSOON. Well, I'm glad there was nobody around to witness that little scene. For the honour of our fellow patients and all that. Craiglockhart Hospital might have succumbed to corporate hysterics.

OWEN. I think I'd have enjoyed seeing that — Edinburgh in apo - p-plexy ... *(OWEN'S attempt at a joke fails. He is near to tears — which are not allowed. He moves away.)*

SASSOON. Look, you're forgetting Mr. Strong's masterpiece.

OWEN. No, I'd never ... *(takes two sheets of blue writing paper from his pocket.)* This ... I didn't *mean* it to be funny, but you never know.

SASSOON. For me?

OWEN. Like everything else. There's a note, too. *(SASSOON is about to unfold the paper.)* But I think I want you to read it after I've gone.

SASSOON. *(putting the paper into his pocket)* Very well.

OWEN. And I'll read this on the train.

SASSOON. As long as you don't shriek with laughter and keep everybody awake. Oh, when you find out what "Grame" is, let me know, will you?

OWEN. "Grame??"

SASSOON. "Grame." Page 17:
"Loud, chiding ewes their lambkins claim;
Can fleec't illusions shrill such *grame*?"

OWEN. I don't believe it. You're making it up.

SASSOON. *(sounding offended)* I am a minor versifier of

the language, not a mass-bloody-murderer of it. Find out
and tell me what the silly man's talking about.

OWEN. I will ... *(about to open the book)* "Grame...?"

SASSOON. You'll miss your train!

OWEN. Yes. *(He puts on his cap.)* Goodbye.

SASSOON. Goodbye.

OWEN. I'll write.

SASSOON. Yes, do. You must. *(suddenly)* Go. Now!

*(OWEN walks away, out of the light. SASSOON is left, sitting in
an armchair. Lights come up on his desk on the other side of the
stage, revealing all of the room for the first time. SASSOON looks
across to the desk, then rises and crosses to it. He picks up some
sheets of manuscript on which he has been working. It is a memoir
of WILFRED OWEN. He starts to read from it.)*

SASSOON. "He did catch the midnight train, fifteen
years ago, on the fourth of November, 1917, when my
dear Wilfred Owen had ... *(He underlines the word.)* "*exactly*
twelve months to live..." *(SASSOON sits at his desk.)* "That
parting would have been easier if we'd had any confidence that either of us would live to meet again. There
wasn't much hope of it. The war in which he and I fought
inspired poetry with the same prodigality with which it
slaughtered the poets. And by 1917, its appetite for death
grew daily by what it fed on." *(He looks across at the chairs
where he and OWEN were sitting.)* But all the same, the parting was harder even than the fear of each other's death ...
I believe that neither of us knew how close that friendship
had become — how much we'd learned to depend on
each other — until we looked at a future apart. *(He takes*

from a desk drawer two sheets of blue paper like the ones OWEN gave him. But these are well-thumbed and the blue has faded. SASSOON reads from the first page.) "You will find something of yourself in this. But everything I do from now on will owe something to you. And of course you'll remember the Shelley, '...One whose spear had pierced me lean'd beside ... and all seemed like some brothers, on a journey wide gone forth, whom now strange meeting did befall in a strange land.' It's not finished. I still have to find a way to reconcile the enemies in death. But this is the best I can give you." *(He turns to the second page.)* " 'Strange friend,' I said, 'here is no cause to mourn.' 'None,' said that other, save the undone years, The hopelessness..."

(Lights reveal OWEN in silhouette upstage. He speaks to SASSOON.)

Owen.
"...Whatever hope is yours
Was my life also; I went hunting wild
After the wildest beauty in the world,
Which lies not calm in eyes or braided hair,
But mocks the steady running of the hour,   ,
And if it grieves, grieves richlier than here.
For by my glee might many men have laughed,
And of my weeping something had been left,
Which must die now. I mean the truth untold,
The pity of war, the pity war distilled..."

(Lights fade out on OWEN. SASSOON carefully refolds the sheets of paper.)

SASSOON. "The pity of war..." I suppose our friendship was almost as unlikely as theirs — that strange meeting between the English and the German soldiers in Hell. But the Hell in which we met was a museum of living horror called, with inappropriate understatement, the Craiglockhart War Hospital for Nervous Disorders. It contained some 150 officers whose minds had been broken by their experience of war. And every night the corridors echoed with their screaming as they relived the war in their dreams. *(He listens. He can still hear it.)* Wilfred was broken in France in the spring of that year. He was accused of cowardice by his Colonel, then sent to Craiglockhart at the end of June — when they didn't know what else to do with him. *(SASSOON looks through some letters from OWEN to his mother.)*

(Lights come up on OWEN, walking as if on his arrival in Edinburgh, 26th June, 1917. OWEN here bears little resemblance to the man in the first scene. He is apprehensive. His moods are extreme and change instantly. His neurasthenic stammer comes with tension, as if his throat had suddenly become paralysed.)

OWEN. My darling Mother, I walked the lovely length of Princes Street. The C-Castle looked more than ever an hallucination with the morning sun behind it.

(Lights reveal a small writing table. OWEN goes to it.)

OWEN. But Craiglockhart Hospital ... well, there's nothing very att-ttractive about that.
SASSOON. For a week he was alone.

OWEN. I have no friends in this place. *(A touch of pride.)* The impulse is not in me to walk abroad and find them.

SASSOON. *(looks at another letter)* Then, his wise doctor persuaded him to become the editor of the Hospital Weekly Journal, "The Hydra." He became active, energetic, even optimistic. And he was writing—

OWEN. *(testing the sound of what he has just written)* "Sing me at morn but only with your laugh;
Even as Spring that laugheth into leaf;
Even as love that laugheth after life..."

SASSOON. He bought a book called "The Old Huntsman" and read some of my poems for the first time.

OWEN. *(very excited)* Dearest Mother, I have just been reading Siegfried Sassoon's new poems, published while I was in France, and I am feeling at a very high pitch of emotion. *N-Nothing* like his trench-life sketches has ever been written, or ever *w-will* be written.

SASSOON. *(looking sceptically at OWEN'S letter)* Well ... Mmmm ...

OWEN. Shakespeare reads vapid after these—

SASSOON. What? "Vapid—??"

OWEN. Not, of course, because Sassoon is the greater artist—

SASSOON. *(relief)* Ah! ... For a moment I wondered.

OWEN. —but because of the subjects. Did you know that he won the Military Cross in the Battle of the Somme last year? There's even a rumor that this year he was recommended for the Victoria Cross. But he was wounded — again — in April and they say he threw his medals into the river. I think he's still convalescing in England.

SASSOON. In that foulest and bloodiest of wars, the worst wound was the Battle of Passchendaele. It began on the 31st of July, 1917. On that same morning The Times carried a Parliamentary Report. *(SASSOON looks at a newspaper clipping. OWEN reads from a similar one.)*

OWEN. "AN OFFICER AND NERVE-SHOCK.
Mr. Lees Smith, Member of Parliament, said that 2/Lt Sassoon, of 3rd Royal Welch Fusiliers who, in the course of the war had been wounded and had gained the Military Cross for gallantry, had handed him a copy of a letter which he had written to his Commanding Officer. 'I am making this statement as an act of wilful defiance of military authority—

SASSOON. *(He stands, as if facing the Tribunal.)* —because I believe that this war is being delibe · ely prolonged by those who have the power to end it ... The war upon which I entered as a war defence and liberation, has now become a war of aggression and conquest ... I have seen and endured the suffering of the troops, and I can no longer be a party to prolonging those sufferings for ends which I believe to be evil and unjust ... Fighting men are being sacrificed, and I make this protest against the deception which is being practised upon them ... Also, I believe, it may help to destroy the callous complaisance with which the majority of those at home regard the continuance of agonies — which they do not share, and which they have not sufficent imagination to realise. S. Sassoon. July 1917.'

OWEN. After receiving this letter, his Commanding Officer forced him to appear before a medical board. They informed him that he must be suffering from the effects of a passing nervous shock, and therefore they would send him to a hospital for officers suffering from mental ailments ... The fact was that the decision was made, not on the grounds of health, but to avoid that *publicity* which any other measure might have had..."

SASSOON. It was all very ingenious. Instead of the Court Martial I'd hoped for, I was sent to Craiglockhart — to swell the ranks of Doctor Rivers' Mentally Disabled. *(SASSOON, angrily, takes off his jacket and puts on a hospital dressing gown. He stands there, glowering. OWEN, in contrast, sounds delighted.)*

OWEN. Dearest Mother, The most exciting news! Siegfried Sassoon has been sent to Craiglockhart! *(picking up five books)* I have bought several copies of "The Old Huntsman." One of them is for you. I'll take them with me and ask him to sign them — when I eventually work up enough courage to knock at his door.

(OWEN, timidly, knocks. SASSOON does not welcome the intrusion. He quickly takes a golf club and a polishing rag from the golf bag, then moves away. SASSOON speaks sharply and does not look at OWEN when he enters the space which is SASSOON'S hospital room.)

SASSOON. Yes? Come! *(OWEN comes forward.)*

(NOTE: In Siegfried's Journey, SASSOON contrasts OWEN at this first meeting with the man who later became a friend. Among the qualities he describes are, "...shyly hesitant..a slight stammer ... a charming honest smile and his manners ... were modest and ingratiating ... He listened eagerly, questioning me with reticent intelligence ... It had taken him two whole weeks ... to muster up

enough courage to approach me...")

OWEN. Lieutenant Sassoon?

SASSOON. For the moment — yes.

OWEN. Oh...

SASSOON. I *am* Sassoon. Is there something you want?

OWEN. I've d-disturbed you. I'm very sorry.

SASSOON. *Having* disturbed me, could you not at least tell me why?

OWEN. It's ... these ...

SASSOON. What are they?

OWEN. Copies of your b-book. Your l-latest book, I mean. "The Old Huntsman." *(SASSOON is surprised, but will not let OWEN see it.)*

SASSOON. Mmm ... Not wise to go around in public with those under your arm. Unless you *want* to stay in this place until the end of the war.

OWEN. No.

SASSOON. No?

OWEN. No — I don't want to stay in this p-place until the end of the war.

SASSOON. Then you'd be safer even with Shelley. And positively impregnable with Rupert Brooke.

OWEN. I really have disturbed you. F-forgive me. Sorry. *(OWEN smiles apologetically and turns to go.)*

SASSOON. No, stay ... ! I don't *mean* to be rude.

OWEN. Oh, it's not rude. I understand.

SASSOON. You do?

OWEN. Oh, yes.

SASSOON. It's just that — in this place, you never know who's going to come in next.

OWEN. Or what m-may be wrong with him.

SASSOON. Exactly. *(A truce seems to be established. OWEN ventures further in.)*

OWEN. Actually, I like Shelley.

SASSOON. *(with no memory of having mentioned him)* Shelley?

OWEN. Almost as much as Keats.

SASSOON. *(blank)* Oh?

OWEN. I'm sorry — I thought — er, I'm sorry.

SASSOON. What, for liking Shelley and Keats?

OWEN. For d-disagreeing with you.

SASSOON. You think I *don't* like Shelley and Keats.

OWEN. Well, I thought you said ... *(thinks)* I'm *sure* you said ... *(SASSOON puts down the golf club, turns to OWEN and challenges him.)*

SASSOON.

"He is made one with Nature...

He is a presence to be felt and known

In darkness and in light, from herb and stone...

He is a portion of the loveliness

Which once he made more lovely..."

OWEN. Yes ... "Adonaïs."

SASSOON. Yes, now give me — just *one* — copy of that, for a moment. *(OWEN, bewildered, hands him a copy of "The Old Huntsman." SASSOON reads from "The Last Meeting," making points unemotionally.)*

"He was beside me now, as swift as light.

I knew him crushed to earth in scentless flowers,

And lifted in the rapture of dark pines.

'For now,' he said, 'my spirit has more eyes

Than heaven has stars; and they are lit by love.

My body is the magic of the world,
And dawn and sunset flame with my spilt blood...' "
*(SASSOON stops. Emotionally unable to go on, he looks and
sounds impassive.)*

OWEN. "The Last Meeting"... *(SASSOON nods, expressionless.)* I should have seen that. Of course. Will you
go on?

SASSOON. No.

OWEN. I think it is profoundly ... It's among the finest
in the book.

SASSOON. Oh, I've written worse — very often.

OWEN. *Won't* you finish reading it?

SASSOON. There's no need. The point is surely made.
Still think I don't like Shelley?

OWEN. That was very stupid of 1..e, I should have
known. With "Adonaïs" above all.

SASSOON. You weren't being at all stupid. It is just
possible that I was being aggressive.

OWEN. *(mildly, defending him)* Or defensive.

SASSOON. *(surprised)* Or — that — as you say. Whatever
else it was, it was rudeness. I ... I hope you'll forgive me.
*(SASSOON returns the golf club to the bag and takes out another.
Returning, he risks a glance at OWEN, who is smiling shyly but
reassuringly at him.)* Now, I don't want to pry, but are you
going to tell me why you're carrying all those copies of
my book about with you? Are you delivering them to the
patients? Has it been made recommended reading? If it
has, the staff must be madder than the inmates. *(OWEN,
enjoying the sense of humour, shakes his head in response.)*
Then why?

OWEN. I wondered if you might inscribe them for
me.

SASSOON. What, all of them?

OWEN. Oh, if it's too much trouble...

SASSOON. No, it's not that. You've contributed at least two shillings' worth of royalties there. But all of them — for you?

OWEN. Oh, no. For friends. And my mother.

SASSOON. I see.

OWEN. And *one* for me.

SASSOON. Good.

OWEN. Then you will?

SASSOON. I'm very flattered. Of course I will.

OWEN. Thank you.

SASSOON. Well, hand them over. *(OWEN does so, then starts searching his pockets.)*

OWEN. I've made a list. *(SASSOON has opened a book and seen "Absolution.")*

SASSOON. Oh, dear God...

OWEN. Sorry...?

SASSOON. This thing:

"War is our scourge, yet war has made us wise
And fighting for our freedom, we are free..."

OWEN. Er ... "Absolution"?

SASSOON. You know, I think if *I* read this one first, I'd be sick all over it then throw it into the fire.

OWEN. Well, I did wonder if you really meant it.

SASSOON. Oh, I meant it when I wrote it, God help me. The truth was revealed a bit more gradually.

OWEN. But you decided to publish it...?

SASSOON. Yes. Bait them with this, and the "Huntsman." Hook them with the rest.

OWEN. Sorry...?

SASSOON. *(patiently)* It's called tactics. They'll never take it in if I just call them fools. But they might if I admit how much of a fool I was myself.

OWEN. Oh, yes I see. It's much harder to win the medal than to throw it away. *(SASSOON is surprised — and suspicious of how much OWEN knows, he demands harshly:)*

SASSOON. What makes you say that?

OWEN. *(his nervousness returning)* It's just that you have to win the m-medal, first — before you have the right to say anything ... *(struggling)* You have to try to write a poem before you can say 'any fool can write poetry.' That's all.

SASSOON. Mmm...

OWEN. About the next one — 'To my Brother'... *(SASSOON turns the page and does not like what he sees.)* When did he — ? I hope you won't mind me asking — but when was he killed?

SASSOON. Two years ago. Exactly two years ago. Gallipoli.

OWEN. Oh ... I suppose that was when most of us began to doubt.

SASSOON. But not me, it would seem ... It was on that peninsula that Hecuba, after the fall of Troy, blinded King Polymestor, slaughtered his children, and was turned into a dog for her pains. Did you know that?

OWEN. No, I didn't.

SASSOON. It could have been an omen — if only they'd known. Elementary Greek should be a compulsory qualification for Ministers of War. *(OWEN is about to laugh, then wonders if SASSOON means it to be funny.)* And, when we crept, humiliated, off that sorry place, at the end of the

year — in the middle of the night — the bedraggled rem-
nants were packed off for a fresh chance to be
slaughtered on the Somme. *(trying to lighten the mood)* Are
you sending one of these to your Colonel, by any chance?
*(But OWEN does not respond to the attempt. His reflex is a sud-
den tension, turning his head away as if ashamed. It is his turn to
wonder how much SASSOON knows.)* What is it? ... I've said
something tactless. Something that hurt? *(no reply)* About
your Colonel? ... Was it your Colonel who had you
sent here?

OWEN. *(mumbling)* Yes ... It — it's not important. *(SAS-
SOON is angry with himself, but then asks for the list of names
with surprising gentleness.)*

SASSOON. Let me see, then. *(takes the list from OWEN)*
Who's this? A relation?

OWEN. That's ... S-Susan is my m-m-mother. *(SAS-
SOON starts to write.)*

SASSOON. That's good. But you surprise me. These
puny attempts at enlightening the civilians — won't they
worry her? Perhaps frighten her.

OWEN. You've said n-nothing there that I've not
already told her in my letters.

SASSOON. Really? You've told her? Was that a good
idea, do you think?

OWEN. She wants the truth. She doesn't want me to
protect her from it. And I certainly couldn't lie to her.

SASSOON. A civilian who wants the truth? Is there such
an animal? Even — *(He finds 'They' in the book.)* this sort
of truth?

"The Bishop tells us when the boys come back
They will not be the same: for they'll have fought

In a just cause...
We're none of us the same! the boys reply.
For George lost both his legs; and Bill's stone blind;
Poor Jim's shot through the lungs and like to die;
And Bert's gone syphilitic: you'll not find
A chap who's served that hasn't found *some* change.
And the Bishop said: The ways of God are strange!

OWEN. That's brilliant. And it's true.

SASSOON. Well, it's true. But for your mother?

OWEN. Yes.

SASSOON. You can trust her with knowing all that?

OWEN. *She* must not be taken in by the lies.

SASSOON. I see. And would you risk telling her about yourself? That, in the end, every one of us can kill and go on killing, if it means saving our own lives?

OWEN. If you love someone, that person has to know *all* that you are. The worst, the most horrific ... And the most shameful.

SASSOON. Everything the war calls out of us, in fact.

OWEN. You know. Of course you do. Better than anybody, I think. It's your poems that will help me to make her understand. Sometime, she will have to know who I really am.

SASSOON. But most of the people at home don't want to know — and they don't even try to imagine.

OWEN. I told you, I wrote to her — even about winter at the Front. Last February. You remember? The cold that makes your brain ache with it? When you're afraid that your eyes will freeze over? I told her about No Man's Land under snow — like the face of the moon, a chaos. I called it a place of madness, where nothing lived — not an insect, not a blade of grass. Only the shadows of the hawks across the sky, when they scent carrion. I said that we were the carrion. The 'Glorious Dead,' lying unburied day after day, until their putrefied bodies explode in our faces. We know that we'll die like that, filthy and terrified. And that *is* how we die. And it's all for lies. Their Justice and Liberation are *lies*. We really die because no one *cares* to save us. No one dares to imagine how it really is.

SASSOON. We are the only ones who can help them to imagine. If they know the truth, the killing will have to stop!

OWEN. Will you ... Will you teach me the words? *(SAS-SOON, having got so near, reacts in character by ducking away.)*

SASSOON. Jingles, that's all I can write ... But until there's something better, let the jingles ring out.

OWEN. You know that's not true. Your poems have too much of yourself in them.

SASSOON. *(surprised, wary)* I'm not sure I want to know what you mean.

OWEN. Compassion is the most important thing.

SASSOON. You can't be serious.

OWEN. It's true. It's here. *(OWEN takes a book from SASSOON'S hands. He finds 'The Death Bed,' which he knows by heart, and starts it, as a challenge. SASSOON, uneasily, moves away from him.)*

"He drowsed and was aware of silence heaped
Round him, unshaken as the steadfast walls;
Aqueous like floating rays of amber light,
Soaring and quivering in the wings of sleep.
Silence and safety; and his mortal shore

Lipped by the inward, moonless waves of death.

Someone was holding water to his mouth.
He swallowed, unresisting; moaned and dropped
Through crimson gloom to darkness; and forgot
The opiate throb and ache that was his wound...
   SASSOON. *(remembering the event, relives it)*
He stirred, shifting his body; then the pain
Leapt like a prowling beast, and gripped and tore
His groping dreams with grinding claws and fangs.
  But someone was beside him; soon he lay
  Shuddering because the evil thing had passed.
  And death, who'd stepped toward him, paused and
  stared.
Light many lamps and gather round his bed.
Lend him your eyes, warm blood, and will to live.
Speak to him; rouse him; you may save him yet.
He's young; he hated War; how should he die
When cruel old campaigners win safe through?

But death replied: 'I choose him.' So he went,
And there was silence in the summer night;
Silence and safety; and the veils of sleep.
Then, far away, the thudding of the guns."
   OWEN. I've been trying for three years to ... Nothing.
Well, never mind ... Would you call that a "jingle?"
   SASSOON. *(a reluctant concession)* There's always one
exception. Sometimes two ... But now, one last book.
*(SASSOON takes the book OWEN is holding, and looks at the
list.)* Who is this one for?
   OWEN. For me.

SASSOON. Of course. *(about to write, then:)* I'm sorry, I don't know your name.

OWEN. Owen. W.E.S. Owen.

SASSOON. *(writing)* W.E.S. Owen ... from ... Well. There you are. *(SASSOON hands over the pile of books.)*

OWEN. *(suddenly formal)* Thank you, for doing that. But thank you more for what's in the book.

SASSOON. The pleasure was mine. The ... astonishment was mine, also. *(OWEN starts to go.)* Lieutenant Owen!

OWEN. Sir?

SASSOON. Who are you?

OWEN. ...Sir?

SASSOON. *What* are you? What do you do?

OWEN. Nothing, now. But I shall be a poet. *(OWEN leaves him, goes straight to his writing table, picks up a pen and speaks urgently.)* My dear Mother, Here is your signed copy of Sassoon's book. I want you to send me all the manuscript verse of mine that's in your keeping!

SASSOON. *(Smiling at OWEN'S reaction to their first meeting, goes to his deak and looks at OWEN'S letter to his mother.)* It's curious to remember now ... I wondered if he'd be any good. He was shy, he was ordinary — provincial, perhaps. But he was ... ardent! And, despite his shyness, there was something ... When he talked about No Man's Land under snow ... I wanted very much to talk to him again. But, in truth *I* was shy of *him*. *(SASSOON leaves the desk, takes off the dressing gown and hangs it up.)*

OWEN. *(OWEN takes a dozen loose manuscript sheets inside the covers of an old school exercise book and crosses towards SASSOON'S room. He knocks on a table.)* Er ... Sassoon?

(Hearing the voice, SASSOON'S shyness gets the better of him. He snatches a letter from his desk and is instantly immersed in it. OWEN steps into the room and stands there, uncertainly.)

SASSOON. Bloody man ... !

OWEN. Who? Me? *(SASSOON seems surprised to see him there.)*

SASSOON. You? ... No, not you. H.G. Wells. Writes in pink ink. *Dim* pink ink. Can't make out a word of it. Looks like, "Hope you'll soon demote yourself to the ... Seal Business in Fife ..." He's gone raving mad. No, wait ... "*Devote* yourself to the *real* business of *life* ..." Oh, I see! "Which is only poetry by the way." Yes...

OWEN. What *is* the "real business of life?"

SASSOON. Politics, of course. He's taken to the Russian Revolution in rather a big way. Expects me to become a sort of Kerensky of the Packlestone Hunt. *(OWEN had been assuming an air of intent seriousness, but that catches him unawares. He snorts with laughter. SASSOON regards him.)*

SASSOON. I think you, probably, have a very silly sense of humour.

OWEN. Sorry.

SASSOON. What is that you're holding? *(OWEN hands him the school exercise book.)*

OWEN. For you. I hoped you might help me.

SASSOON. ...To write a school essay? *(SASSOON, dubious, opens the book. OWEN points to the first poem.)*

OWEN. That one, 'The Dead Beat,' I wrote after reading yours.

SASSOON. Oh...? *(OWEN moves away while SASSOON reads it. He finds an object on the desk of consuming interest. He*

starts to hum the refrain of 'They wouldn't believe me.' SASSOON
is acutely aware of all this activity.) First he steals my style,
then he ruins my favourite song.

OWEN. Sorry. Well...?

SASSOON. Well ... You could find a better model than
me. And this middle bit:
"Not that the Kaiser frowns imperially.
He sees his wife, how cosily she chats..."

OWEN. Oh, that's old.

SASSOON. Well, it hasn't improved with keeping, has
it? And it really doesn't work with the first and last stan-
zas, now does it? *(SASSOON hands it back. OWEN returns to*
his own room and tears up the page.)

OWEN. Dear Mother, It's no good. *(SASSOON has read*
another and calls out.)

SASSOON. Owen? Wilfred? *(OWEN goes quickly back to*
him.) I do like this one. It's charming.
"Sing me at morn but only with your laugh;
Even as Spring that laugheth into leaf..."
A perfect piece of work. Yes ... Do me a copy. I'll show it
around. *(SASSOON gives it to him then reads another. OWEN*
goes back, glowing.)

OWEN. My dear Mother, A short lyric has been pro-
nounced "perfect."

SASSOON. "Rich odoured flowers, so whelmed in fetid
earth..." Oh, dear... *(SASSOON puts the offending poem away.)*

OWEN. P.S.! Some old sonnets of mine didn't please
him at all.*(SASSOON takes out a poem which is between a folded*
sheet of blank paper.)

SASSOON. "To Eros.
In that I loved you, Love, I worshipped you;
(OWEN, hearing this, comes back. He is nervous and em-
barrassed.)

In that I worshipped well, I sacrificed.
All of most worth I bound and burnt and slew..."
It's ... what? Luscious, perhaps? A bit sweet for my
tooth...

OWEN. I didn't know that was in there... *(OWEN holds
out his hand for it. SASSOON notices his embarrassment.)*

SASSOON. Inside that folded sheet. Shouldn't I have
seen it? Oh ... I'm extremely sorry. *(Handing it back, he
notices the final lines.)* Wait ... !
"... Starkly I returned
To stare upon the ash of all I burned."
Now *that's* strong. Do you know, it is there. There is
something. But ... Oh, you've got a lot of work to do.
Don't think about publishing. Not yet. Leave that. For
now, you just sweat your guts out writing poetry. *(OWEN
gratefully takes the poem and starts to go back.)*

OWEN. My dear Mother, The last thing Sassoon said to
me was, "Sweat your guts out writing ..."

SASSOON. Wilfred?? Where *are* you?? *(OWEN returns.)* I
do wish you wouldn't keep running away, old chap.
Now, *this:*
"Out there, we've walked quite friendly up to Death;
Sat down and eaten with him, cool and bland, —
Pardoned his spilling mess-tins in our hand.
We've sniffed the green thick odour of his breath..."
(SASSOON stops and stares at the paper.)

OWEN. Not too sweet for you?

SASSOON. Are there ... others, like this? *(OWEN searches
his pockets.)*

OWEN. Well, I've been trying to do something
about this.

SASSOON. What is it?

OWEN. I think it has to be called, 'Exposure.' *(OWEN finds the poem. SASSOON offers him a chair.)*

SASSOON. Go on.

OWEN. But it's ... it's not finished!

SASSOON. *Go on!! (OWEN sits and very reluctantly starts to read. He is acutely self-conscious and does the poem less that justice.)*

OWEN.

"Our brains ache, in the merciless iced east winds that knive us...

Wearied we keep awake because the night is silent...

Low, drooping flares confuse our memory of the
    salient...

Worried by silence, sentries whisper, curious, nervous,
    But nothing happens."

(SASSOON realising he has made OWEN nervous takes the poem from him and reads it himself. His more measured pace is right for it, but the poem keeps taking him by surprise.)

SASSOON.

"Pale flakes with fingering stealth come feeling for
    our faces—

We cringe in holes, back on forgotten dreams, and
    stare, snow-dazed,

Deep into grassier ditches. So we drowse, sun-dozed,

Littered with blossoms trickling where the blackbird
    fusses,

— Is it that we are dying?

Slowly our ghosts drag home: glimpsing the sunk
    fires..."?

OWEN. I can't finish that, yet. The 'dozed' rhyme ... And it's ... Well, I think the next stanza is the final one.

SASSOON.
"To-night, this frost will fasten on this mud and us,
Shrivelling many hands, puckering foreheads crisp.
The burying party, picks and shovels in shaking grasp,
Pause over half-known faces. All their eyes are ice,
     But nothing happens."
(OWEN waits for a comment, then nervously breaks the silence himself.)

OWEN. It was last winter. February. My first in France. The poem is almost as hard as that was ... To finish, I mean.

SASSOON. *(He is astonished by the poem but makes a good attempt at sounding casual.)* I'll gladly have a word with Heinemann. But I think Martin Secker is the publisher for a small volume — say, ten or twenty poems. I'll get in touch with them right away. *(SASSOON hands him the poems. OWEN returns to his room and sits.)*

OWEN. My own dear Mother, These last days have been the fullest, the happiest of the year. I like Sassoon equally as a man, as a friend, as a poet — and his new poems are superb beyond anything in his last book. *And,* he seems to have ⌐hanged his mind about me not publishing yet. He thinks he can help me. *(SASSOON is back at his desk.)*

SASSOON. I have an uncomfortable suspicion that I was a bit slow in recognising his ... exceptional quality. But I'm thankful I seem not to have discouraged him.

OWEN. Sassoon's praise is the greatest possible encouragement I could hope for. He is already a closer friend to me than any. But, of course, I don't tell him. He is very English in these matters.

SASSOON. As a rule, he was reticent, retiring — the quiet one. But it is also true that there was sometimes an ... intensity of emotion in him, and more often in his poetry, which I found almost ... shocking. Well ... During all the rest of our time together at Craiglockhart, and I was with him every day, he was almost always cheerful — and he was busy. *(SASSOON puts on his jacket. OWEN approaches him with proofs of 'The Hydra.')*

OWEN. Siegfried, I want a favour.

SASSOON. A small one?

OWEN. An enormous one.

SASSOON. I'm playing golf.

OWEN. I want 'Dreamers' for the next issue of the journal. Please?

SASSOON. Oh, all right. *(SASSOON finds the poem in a folder and gives it to him. OWEN starts to go.)* Wait ... As long as you put in one of yours. That lovely thing: "Sing me at morn but only with your laugh" ...

OWEN. Oh, no. Not next to one of yours.

SASSOON. *(taking back 'Dreamers')* Then you won't have one of mine to put it next to.

OWEN. But I can't put my own poems in — I'm the editor!

SASSOON. I'm not impressed.

OWEN. Well, it would have to be an-anonymous...

SASSOON. As long as it goes in. Then I can send copies off to people who might help.

OWEN. *(alarmed)* Copies of *my* poem?

SASSOON. *(thrusting 'Dreamers' at him) Do* it! *(OWEN moves away, doubtfully. SASSOON seems pleased with himself.)* And so it was through blackmail that a poem by Wilfred Owen was, for the first time, seen it print. *(SASSOON goes to get his golf bag. OWEN, now cheerful, returns with a new set of proofs.)*

OWEN. Siegfried! A favour?

SASSOON. No. It's my turn.

OWEN. Do you remember saying we could have 'Rear Guard' ... *(stops) Your* turn?

SASSOON. Meet a friend of mine. At the station. He's coming up specially to see me.

OWEN. Well, all right — although I'm ... Why can't you meet him yourself?

SASSOON. I'm playing golf! Bring him up to the course when he arrives. *(SASSOON starts to go.)*

OWEN. Er ... Wait! Who is he? How will I know him?

SASSOON. Graves, Robert, Captain, Poet. Big chap. Curly hair, broken nose. You probably won't like him very much. *(thinks about it)* Not sure he'll take to you. *(SASSOON goes upstage into the shadow. OWEN sits at his table.)*

OWEN. My own dear Mother, On Saturday, I met Robert Graves — for Sassoon, whom nothing could keep from his morning's golf. I took Graves over to the golf course when he arrived. He is a big, rather plain fellow. Siegfried showed him my longish war-piece, 'Disabled.' *(OWEN picks up a letter from Graves. SASSOON, returning from the course, passes OWEN'S room.)* Siegfried ... ! Graves has just written to me.

SASSOON. Good. *(SASSOON starts to go on his way again.)*

OWEN. But *look* at it! *(SASSOON reluctantly returns.)*

SASSOON. If I must ... "Do you know, Owen, that's a damn fine poem of yours, that 'Disabled.' Really, *damn* fine! So good, the general weight and sound of the words that the occasional metrical outrages ... are most surprising. It's like seeing a golfer drive on to the green in *one,* and then use a cleek instead of a putter and hole out in *twelve...*"

OWEN. What's he talking about? *(SASSOON is concerned that OWEN may be taking it too seriously. He tries to make up for Graves's lack of tact.)*

SASSOON. He means he thinks you start very well —but after that you go, ever so slightly, to pieces.

OWEN. "Cleeks" instead of "putters?"

SASSOON. You don't know anything at all about golf, do you? Nothing at all?

OWEN. No, not really. Far too provincial, you see.

SASSOON. *That's* no excuse!

OWEN. Oh? You mean I can't blame my boring, Shropshire, middle-class, or whatever I am, upbringing?

SASSOON. Nothing whatever to do with it. And don't blame your father for being a railwayman, either.

OWEN. An Assistant Superintendent of the Great Western, please.

SASSOON. Whether he's railwayman, a dustman, or the Governor General of Southern Rhodesia, it's no possible excuse for your appalling ignorance about anything to do with sport.

OWEN. The truth, then?

SASSOON. We tell each other nothing but truth. That's been decided. Remember?

OWEN. The truth, then ... I think it's a boring game. *(SASSOON, shocked, stares at him with profound pity.)*

SASSOON. Oh, my poor, dear chap. *(SASSOON returns to his own room. OWEN follows.)*

OWEN. Sorry...

SASSOON. No, I'm sorry — for you. You're so single-minded, you'll burn yourself to ashes before you're thirty.

OWEN. I suppose I'd better make the most of the next six years, then.

SASSOON. Yes! *(The same thought crosses their minds, but SASSOON goes to hang up his golf bag and OWEN says, brightly:)*

OWEN. You were going to tell me about cleeks and putters, sir.

SASSOON. Ah, yes. Well, if you use a cleek instead of a putter, it's like ... *(Seeing OWEN'S face, he wants to soften the blow.)* Well, it's like ... er ...

OWEN. You don't really know yourself, do you?

SASSOON. It's like using a sledge-hammer to crack a nut! *(OWEN is suddenly crestfallen.)*

OWEN. Oh ... I'm being too heavy-handed again, is that it?

SASSOON. Well possibly too heavy-handed for Robert. But it's not *all* bad ... *(takes the letter from OWEN)* How about this? "My *violent* pleasure at some of the lines"...

OWEN. *Some* of them...

SASSOON. Oh, come on, old chap. And *then* he says, "Owen, you have seen things; you are a poet!"

OWEN. And *then* he says...?

SASSOON. "But you're a very careless one at present."
Oh ...You know, Robert always was a bit dogmatic. One
night, after we'd been to a concert, he took my breath
away by declaring that Beethoven's Fifth was "nothing,
compared with the Bonny Earl o' Moray..." I wouldn't
worry too much about it, if I were you. Beethoven seems
to have survived.

OWEN. Oh, I'm not worried...

SASSOON. *(hoping to find a compliment in the letter)* "I have
no doubt at all that if you turned seriously to writing—"

OWEN. *Seriously?!*

SASSOON. Oh, shush! "—you could obtain Parnassus
in no time, while I'm still struggling on the knees of that
stubborn peak." ... Does Parnassus have knees? "Till
then good luck in the good work. Yours, Robert Graves.
Love to Sassoon."

OWEN. Well ... ? What do you think?

SASSOON. I think Robert is the sort of man one likes
better ... after he has left the room *(But OWEN still refuses
to smile.) I'm* still smarting from when he described fox-
hunting as the sport of "snobs and half-wits." But he's a
fine poet. He's an original. It's just that you and he live in
different worlds, that's all. *(SASSOON gives him the letter
and goes to put on his trench coat. OWEN takes this as a dismissal
and goes back to his room. SASSOON does not see him go — he is
using the trench coat as an excuse not to look at him while he pays a
tortuous compliment.)* And he's absolutely right about you
reaching the top of Mount Parnassus, whether it has
knees or not. I think he might reach it. I sometimes think

I can't even see the summit, let alone get there. But you ...
Oh, you, I think, could show all of us the way! If you
don't go too far ahead of us — *(SASSOON looks up,
anticipating OWEN'S pleasure.)* Oh, he's gone! Pity. That
was the first real compliment I've ever paid him. What a
waste of all that effort...

*(Lights start to fade down to the desk area. SASSOON takes his
army cap from the hatstand, looks at it, remembering.)*

SASSOON. October, 1917. The middle of the afternoon.
The deep yellow sunshine of a Scottish autumn. I'd been
out on the course. Constant practice was improving my
game, I was feeling pleased with myself. And then, in the
club house, I heard the latest news from Passchendaele.
There had been a new Offensive — the biggest yet. *(He is
suddenly angry. He jams the cap on his head and strides across to
OWEN's room.)*

(Lights up quickly on OWEN, working at his table.)

SASSOON. Wilfred!
OWEN. You're back early. Did you have a good
game?
SASSOON. I hit an absolutely perfect tee-shot up the
fairway to the first green.
OWEN. Is that good? Well done ... Then why are you
looking so angry?
SASSOON. Come out with me to Milnathort.
OWEN. Now?
SASSOON. Now!

OWEN. The Thistle?
SASSOON. Yes. Or to walk. *Come on!* Please...?
OWEN. Of course I will.

(OWEN grabs his cap and follows him, puzzled. They walk in silence, upstage. Lights suggest evening sunshine, through trees. The "Peewit" cry of a lapwing may be heard. OWEN is very concerned, but waits until SASSOON comes to a stop before he says, gently:)

OWEN. Siegfried ... Tell me?
SASSOON. When is it that you come up in front of the Board?
OWEN. Oh, is that it? ... A week's time. The 28th.
SASSOON. Will you be passed fit? For General Service?
OWEN. I think so. I *am* fit.
SASSOON. Oh ... ? And the dreams?
OWEN. Sometimes.
SASSOON. Always the same?
OWEN. Yes, Savy Wood. After I'd been blown up. *(He starts to see it.)* Lying in the crater. Lieutenant G-Gaukroger in bits around me.
SASSOON. Oh, Christ! ... Wilfred—
OWEN. No, it's all right. Only sometimes, now. It's because I was there for two days, expecting to die with him. It will take time for that to go away. But since you and I met — talked — since you began to help — I *can* go through a whole night without thinking about it.
SASSOON. So you'll tell them you're fit. And you'll go back?
OWEN. The d-doctor thinks I should get something

lighter for a few months. Then I'll have to decide whether I c-can try again. *(OWEN, aware that the return of the stammer is giving him the lie, is unprepared for SASSOON'S attack.)*

SASSOON. Don't you *know* what's happening at Passchendaele?

OWEN. You've heard something?

SASSOON. It's the worst yet. We've lost a quarter of a million — or more.

OWEN. God...

SASSOON. It sounds as if half of them are being drowned in the mud.

OWEN. God help them...

SASSOON. The new tanks, even the big guns are being swallowed up by it.

OWEN. They've got to stop now — surely?

SASSOON. Lloyd George has already tried, but Haig goes on and on — and we gain nothing! We are there only to kill Germans. And ourselves. And you'll go back, for *that?*

OWEN. If I'm sent—

SASSOON. There are ways of getting round it, you know.

OWEN. But if they send me, how could I get round it? ... Oh, I don't know ... But I can't speak — I can't shout any kind of protest until I've earned the right. I need some ... reputation. You already have that.

SASSOON. Oh, please, Wilfred!

OWEN. You have! It was the medals you threw into the river, not the courage that won them.

SASSOON. More like lunacy...

OWEN. Well, they sent me here because they thought I

was a coward.

SASSOON. And you know they were wrong!

OWEN. No, Siegfried, I don't! I can't be *sure.* I'll never be sure as long as I stay here. I've got to go back and face it sometime.

SASSOON. And get yourself killed? *Why?* Because those fools only believe in the wounds they can see?

OWEN. No, it's not just for them. *(His distress is growing.)* I've got to know for myself. It touches everything I do. Every line I write about the war — I think, sometimes, all I'm trying to do is justify myself.

SASSOON. For what? ... *They've* made you think like that.

OWEN. Yes. But what if they're right? It was my first time — and I couldn't stop thinking about how he died.

SASSOON. And that you might die the same way?

OWEN. Yes.

SASSOON. That's what terrifies all of us!

OWEN. But it didn't stop you, did it?

SASSOON. That's not the point—

OWEN. It is. It's why they listen to you. They know your protest had nothing to do with cowardice.

SASSOON. Wilfred, *they* wanted to turn me into a hero. Don't you try to do the same thing. There were times when I was so frightened I thought I was paralysed.

OWEN. But all they can see are medals and scars.

SASSOON. It's not only the scars on the outside — !

OWEN. Yes! I know I'm neurotic, but I'm no longer neurasthenic! *(OWEN moves violently away.)*

SASSOON. I didn't mean ... You *know* I didn't mean ... !

(SASSOON, realising he has failed, stands apart, his back to

OWEN. There is a silence. When OWEN looks up and sees him, he is more concerned for SASSOON than for himself.)

OWEN. You know, you've still not told me. If you hit a perfect tee-shot, or whatever it is, why were you so angry?

SASSOON. Well, it can't go on forever, can it? I heard about Passchendaele ... Oh, Wilfred, I've no right to be here!

OWEN. Right? They sent you here to keep you quiet.

SASSOON. I was woken up last night. There was a man sobbing outside my bedroom door. I went to see what was happening. He was crouched on the floor, half naked, shivering with cold, crying like a child. When I tried to lift him up he grabbed at me. All I could see in his eyes was pure hate. He hated me because he could see I wasn't mad ... Well, if I'm not mad, I have no right to be here. I'm "shortening the war" for myself, "making a separate peace." And what does that make me?

OWEN. It's the same thing, isn't it? The same as me ... *(SASSOON had not seen it. It silences him.)* Let's go on. I'd like a drink.

SASSOON. All right ... I promise not to tell your mother you've broken the pledge.

OWEN. Come on. *(They move to an area of moonlight. SAS-SOON collects two pint tankards. OWEN sits on a table.)* It's getting dark ... Look! There! A meteor! *(SASSOON does not see the "meteor." Stillness, quiet.)* I don't know where either of us will go. But I'm glad I'm here, tonight, with you.

SASSOON. Yes ... It's cold. The winter stars. In Pas-schendaele, the mud will be freezing over them. *(OWEN stares at him. Then he takes his notebook and pencil from his pocket.)*

Owen. Siegfried ... ?

Sassoon. Mmmm?

Owen. It should be like a church service. Like a piece of music. Like a blessing. I don't want to call it an Elegy. Give me a word.

Sassoon. You're the one who knows about church services. What about ... 'Anthem?'

Owen. That's it. That's what it needed. *(OWEN writes the word. SASSOON'S curiosity gets the better of him. He looks over OWEN'S shoulder at the poem.)*

Sassoon. "For," not "to."

Owen. What?

Sassoon. You can't have an Anthem "to." Anthem "for."

Owen. Oh, yes. Thank you.

Sassoon. Why don't you try "monstrous" — there? "Bells" are solemn. "Guns" — monstrous.

Owen. Er ... yes. Better.

Sassoon. That line, there. You've lost the irony, haven't you? Prayers aren't "music." If you tried ... "mockeries" ... it would incorporate everything else: prayers, bells — choirs.

Owen. Good. Thank you.

Sassoon. What's the problem *here? (SASSOON takes the book from him. In the penultimate line, correction is piled on top of correction.)*

Owen. I think it has to echo the long "i's": shine, goodbyes, minds, blinds and the rest. I wondered about "sweet white" ...?

SASSOON. Good for a glass of wine. Doesn't add much to "minds," does it?

OWEN. I had "silent," before.

SASSOON. Oh, yes, that's better ... But ... You've got enough long "i's" there. Wouldn't it be better still if you could say *why* they were silent?

OWEN. Well, yes — but how?

SASSOON. ..."Patient?" It would give you the alliteration with "pallor" and "pall."

OWEN. Yes. *(OWEN writes it in. SASSOON looks at the end of the poem, then at OWEN with something like wonder.)*

SASSOON. The final line is perfect and beautiful.

OWEN. Thank you.

SASSOON. Now, let me hear all of it.

OWEN. "Anthem for Dead Youth.
What passing-bells for these—"

SASSOON. No ... It's not for those who are dead. It's for the ones who will die — isn't it?

OWEN. Yes. *(He thinks about it, then writes:)*
"Anthem for Doomed Youth.
What passing-bells for these who die as cattle?
    —Only the monstrous anger of the guns.
    Only the stuttering rifles' rapid rattle
Can patter out their hasty orisons.
No mockeries now for them; no prayers nor bells;
    Nor any voice of mourning save the choirs,—
The shrill, demented choirs of wailing shells;
    And bugles calling for them from sad shires.

What candles may be held to speed them all?

Not in the hands of boys, but in their eyes
Shall shine the holy glimmer of good-byes.
The pallor of girls' brows shall be their pall;
Their flowers the tenderness of patient minds,
And each slow dusk a drawing-down of blinds."
(SASSOON raises his tankard and drinks a silent toast. OWEN responds. The silence continues.)

OWEN. Can I take your silence as a sign of approval?

SASSOON. That's the way I always register approval, you know that ... And I know a great poem when I hear one.

OWEN. "Great?"

SASSOON. Dear Wilfred ... You must know about *this* one. *(OWEN says nothing.)* Can I take your silence as a sign of consent? *(OWEN'S response is a broad smile.)* You know, I once paid you a compliment about reaching the summit of Mount Parnassus—

OWEN. Did you? I don't remember.

SASSOON. Be that as it may ... I *did*—

OWEN. No, surely. That was Graves.

SASSOON. You were not there at the time ... but I paid you a compliment, nevertheless.

OWEN. I wish I had been there.

SASSOON. Well, with this Anthem, or Elegy or whatever it's to be called— *(SASSOON looks at him and says very deliberately.)* I think you're at the summit, looking down at the rest of us.

OWEN. Oh, no. I needed too much help to get there — *if* that's where I am — to look down on anyone. I owe so much gratitude, I ... I shall never be able to express it.

SASSOON. You are there because it's your achievement! The "assistants" are not important. You stand there by yourself. *(SASSOON lifts him to his feet, and it brings them, for a moment, very close. But it is too close for SASSOON who, with a gesture of apology, walks away, leaving OWEN standing there. OWEN goes slowly across to collect his cap and pack, while SAS-SOON, upstage of the desk, hangs up his cap and trench coat.)* It was a week later that the Board passed him fit. But only for Light Duties, as yet. He was posted to Scarborough. On his last evening, we had dinner together in a quiet Club in Edinburgh...

(Lights come up on the arm chairs where the opening scene took place. SASSOON crosses and sits in one of them.)

SASSOON. ...and to make him laugh on his journey, I gave him a book of the most ... the most indescribable verse I've ever had the pleasure of laughing at:
"Loud-chiding ewes their lambkins claim:
Can fleec't illusions shrill such *grame?*"
OWEN. I don't believe it. You're making it up.
SASSOON. *(sounding offended)* I am a minor versifier of the language, not a mass-bloody-murderer of it. Find out and tell me what the silly man's talking about.
OWEN. I will ... *(about to open the book)* "Grame" ...?
SASSOON. You'll miss your train!
OWEN. Yes. *(He puts on his cap.)* Goodbye.
SASSOON. Goodbye.
OWEN. I'll write.
SASSOON. Yes, do. You must. *(suddenly)* Go. Now! *(As before, OWEN walks away, out of the light. SASSOON is left sit-*

ting in the arm chair.) Twelve months left ... When he reached home, he wrote to thank me for the brown, sealed envelope I'd given him when we parted. It contained a ten-pound note, and the London address of a very close friend of mine I hoped might help him — my dear Robbie Ross.

(Lights come up fast on OWEN, upstage. He is ablaze with enthusiasm.)

OWEN. My *dear* Sassoon, When I opened your envelope in a quiet corner of the Club staircase, I sat on the stairs and groaned a little, and then I loosed off volumes of an epopt epistle — which I put by, as you would recommend for such effusions, until I could think over the thing without *grame.*

SASSOON. *(to himself)* Yes. But what does the silly word *mean?*

OWEN. I thank you; but not on this paper only, or in any writing. I *imagined* you were entrusting me with some holy secret concerning yourself.

SASSOON. There were, I think, by this time, no secrets between us.

OWEN. But the contents of this envelope have not intensified my feelings for you by the least *grame.*

SASSOON. Oh, I wish now I'd never given him the bloody book...

OWEN. You must know that since mid-September, when you still regarded me as a tiresome little knocker-at-your-door, I held you as KEATS plus CHRIST plus my COMMANDING OFFICER plus my FATHER-

CONFESSOR plus AMENOPHIS IV — in profile. What is all this — mathematically? In effect it is this: that I love you, dispassionately, so much, so *very* much, dear fellow, that the blasting little smile you wear on reading this can't hurt me in the least.

SASSOON. He misjudged me — for once.

OWEN. If you consider what the above names have, severally, done for me, you will know what you are doing. And you have *fixed* my life — however short. You did not *light* me: I was always a mad comet; but you have fixed me. I spun around you, a satellite, for a month, but I shall swing out soon — a dark star in the orbit where you will blaze. Someday, I must tell how we sang, shouted, whistled and danced through the dark lanes of Colinton; and how we laughed till the meteors showered around us, and we fell calm under the winter stars. *(He becomes quieter, more certain.)* And some of us saw the pathway of the spirits for the first time. And seeing that pathway so far above us, and feeling the good road so safe beneath us, we praised God with louder whistling; and knew we loved one another as no men love for long. *(SASSOON leans forward and puts his head in his hands.)* I wish you were less undemonstrative — for I have many adjectives with which to qualify myself. As it is, I can only say I am ... Your *proud* friend, Owen.

(Lights fade on OWEN.)

SASSOON. *(Warmly remembers OWEN'S happiness; the mockery is gentle.)* My "proud friend" had made another hero to worship. It was *one* of his great talents ... But what he called "the pathway of the spirits" was just beginning to take him towards achievements which are still marvellous to me.

(Lights fade out on SASSOON.)

THE END OF ACT ONE

ACT TWO

Darkness.

A band playing a military march. Cheering crowds.

SASSOON'S VOICE.
You smug-faced crowds, who cheer and cheer ...
Sneak home and pray you'll never know
The hell where youth and laughter go.
(Lights have come up on SASSOON, asleep at his desk. A clap of thunder, like an explosion.)

OWEN'S VOICE. Oh, Jesus ... Jesus, make it stop... *(a louder explosion)* Siegfried! Siegfried, make it stop!

SASSOON. *(waking, startled)* Wilfred! *(He realizes where he is.)*
"When I'm asleep, dreaming and lulled and warm,—
They come, the homeless ones, the noiseless dead.
While the dim charging breakers of the storm
Bellow and drone and rumble overhead,
Out of the gloom they gather about my bed.
   They whisper to my heart; their thoughts are mine.
   "Why are you here with all your watches ended?
   From Ypres to Frise we sought you in the Line."
In bitter safety I awake, unfriended;
And while the dawn begins with slashing rain
I think of the Battalion in the mud.
"When are you going out to them again?
Are they not still your brothers through our blood?"

(Lights reveal OWEN, sitting apart.)

OWEN. I sit alone and therefore with you, my dear Siegfried. For that name, more than anything in any envelope you gave me, I give thanks and rejoice. I am very safe here in Scarborough and very busy; but I shall have time for seclusion. There is no-one here whose mind is Truth — or whose body is Keats's synonym for Truth...

SASSOON. Their wrongs are mine ... They died — he died — and mutinous I cried to those who sent him. Love drove me to rebel. Love drives me back, to be with them in hell ... To be forgiven ... *(OWEN rises and looks across to SASSOON.)*

OWEN. Very dear Siegfried, shall I ever be able to thank you? *(OWEN moves nearer and stands behind him.)* I had a Seventh Heaven of a time in London. Robbie took me to the Reform Club for lunch. Next to me sat an odd, upstart rodent of a man — Mr. Arnold Bennett! Opposite me, a pair of bayonet-coloured eyes threatened me from over, as it were, a brown sandbag — Mr. H.G. Wells! H. G. talked to me *exclusively* for an hour! ... And I do wish you could have come to Robert Graves's wedding. I think we might have laughed a little. He wore field-boots, spurs and sword, and Nancy looked pretty in a blue silk dress. But she'd read the Wedding Service for the first time that morning and she was furious: didn't want to obey all that, and refused to have her name changed to Graves. They finally agreed on a very short, modified form of the Service, and when they came to the Responses, Robert roared them and Nancy snapped them out. At the reception we drank Champagne while the bride went off to change. She came back dressed in her Land Girl's uniform: breeches and a smock. Everybody looked a bit surprised ... Among the guests were Max Beer-

bohm, William Heinemann, Edward Marsh — and Robbie introduced me to them all as, "Mr. Owen, a poet." Or
even just as, "Owen, the poet!" ... Oh, Siegfried, what a
world you're making for me! But now, dearest of friends,
write and tell me how you are.

SASSOON. My dear Wilfred, Dr. Rivers tells me that if I
stick to my pacifist statement I shall be kept here until the
end of the war. And so I should join the ranks of the com-
placent ones — the safe ones. Well ... I like the comfort-
able idea of being middle-aged, smoking a pipe and
writing my memoirs. And one day I should like to listen
to Mozart in Salzburg — if Austria still exists after the
war. But those are daydreams. There are other dreams, at
night — "When are you coming back? When are you
going out to them again?" — from the dead as well as the
few survivors. One of the dead more than all the others.
Nothing I've done so far has helped me to live with his
death. I *can't* leave it there ... I won't try to explain. You'll
understand, even though it doesn't make sense.

*(OWEN does not understand and is concerned. Music is heard,
slow and gentle.)*

SASSOON. It will soon be 1918. Let it be the year of
Wilfred Owen! I drink to your triumphs — and to our
memories of Scotland ... *(SASSOON drinks whisky from a
tumbler beside him.)*

OWEN. It is almost midnight: the intolerable instant of
change. Last year at this time, I lay awake in a windy tent
in the middle of a vast, dreadful encampment — a kind
of paddock where the beasts are kept before the

slaughterhouse. I heard the revellings of the Scottish troops, who are now dead — and who knew then that they would be dead. I thought of this present night and whether I should be d ...

(A clock starts to strike midnight.)

OWEN. But I go out of this year a poet. I am started. I feel the great swelling of the open sea taking me! My new poem, 'Miners,' is being published this week in the 'Nation.' Isn't it odd that they've accepted this when they refused our 'Anthem for Doomed Youth' in October? I wish that could have been my first in a real paper. But, of course, I'd not met Robbie then. Do you think he could have said something to the editor? Tell me, have you been passed by the Board? And how do we keep you from France? Oh, I've studied and expanded your sole letter to me until I can make no more of it. I want some more, please!

SASSOON. Very dear Wilfred, I write for the last time from Dottyville. I'm going back. The Board has passed me fit for General Service Overseas — a rare honour on discharge from this place. I rejoin my Regiment this week ... But make no mistake — I have every intention of being extremely active when I'm a ghost. And I shall go on haunting you until you achieve all the great things I expect of you. *(OWEN goes back towards his arm chair.)*

OWEN. My dearest Mother, Siegfried is going back to France. He writes like a condemned man, with just enough time to put everything straight. He has asked all his friends to befriend me — but especially Robbie Ross.

And I can't even write to thank him. I don't know where he is. *(SASSOON rises. He looks through the dates in a diary of his travels.)*

SASSOON. I took the long road back to France — via Limerick, Brindisi, Alexandria and Jerusalem. But we didn't stay in Palestine for long. Within a month, we got news from the Western Front; so bad that we were packed off immediately from Palestine to France. We landed at Marseilles on the 7th of May. My war was starting again. By the 8th of June, I was back in the Front Line. Our mission was to take back those few miles of battered ground we'd bought with half a million lives in those battles of the Somme two years before. I found myself in the same place where I'd been wounded in Easter 1917. Hundreds of thousands of lives had bought *nothing*. Had *proved* nothing! ... I wonder, what was I trying to prove? ... Just that I was not a sheep, waiting to be slaughtered at their command. And nor would I lead my Company to be slaughtered at their command! ... Another protest, I suppose. Even more ineffectual than the first. All I did was go out on a raid — unofficially — And when the sun came up in No Man's Land, it was hot. A beautiful summer morning. I took off my tin hat to feel the sun on my face. And I didn't hear the bullet leave the rifle. One minute, I was revelling in the astonishment of being alive, and the next ... I was lying flat on my face with what felt like a very large hole in the right side of my skull ... They carried me back to England in the middle of July. My war seemed to be over. *(He starts to take off his jacket.)* I couldn't understand why I'd not been killed, when there were so many others who ... It took me a long tome to accept the fact that now I was not going to be killed ... that

I should be one of the survivors ...! *(He brings forward a wheel chair.)* After all that, I was going to live on. To write the Memoirs. *(He takes a vivid, blood-red blanket from the chair, sits and covers his knees with it.)* To listen to Mozart in Salzburg.

(He seems to sleep. Lights up on OWEN, reading a short note. Suddenly he stands, alarmed.)

OWEN. Dear Mother, Siegfried has been shot in the head by a sniper's bullet. They've brought him to London. You'll understand that I must use my leave and go to him. *(Then ,to himself.)* Please God, this time he's done with war. *(OWEN takes a book from the table, Sassoon's newly published 'Counter-Attack,' in a "blood-red and yellow paper cover." He crosses towards SASSOON.)* Siegfried? ... Siegfried, it's me.

SASSOON. What? Mmm? What do you want?

OWEN. It's me. You remember? Wilfred. I've ... come to see you. *(SASSOON frowns, trying to concentrate, uncertain at first whether the figure is real.)*

SASSOON. Oh, yes. My dear chap ... *(OWEN grasps his hand, reassuring him.)* Wilfred ...! Oh, how kind of you ... *(He tries, weakly, to get to his feet.)*

OWEN. Don't try to move.

SASSOON. I'm sorry, I can't seem to stand up, just at the moment. I think I might fall on my head ... I promise you, I've not had a drink for weeks.

OWEN. I shouldn't have woken you. I'm sorry.

SASSOON. Wilfred, please ... Won't you sit down? Find a chair. Sit by me. *(OWEN brings a chair. It slips out of his grasp and falls. SASSOON cries out at the noise.)*

OWEN. I'm sorry. I'm so sorry — I frightened you. *(SASSOON is turned away. There is a moment's pause.)*

SASSOON. Frightened me? ... Why should you think I'd be frightened?

OWEN. No, I just thought I might have startled you, that's all. *(SASSOON struggles to clear his head.)*

SASSOON. Wilfred, listen...

OWEN. Yes?

SASSOON. I'm not mad. My head still ... functions. It — well, it hurts sometimes, so they give me things.

OWEN. Yes.

SASSOON. But underneath all that, I'm still *me.* You remember?

OWEN. I remember.

SASSOON. I'm still .. who I was. Slower, I think, so you may have to be careful. But not *kind.* I think I should find that very embarrassing.

OWEN. You *are* still who you were. *(OWEN'S warm smile reassures him.)*

SASSOON. Good ... That's good. *(OWEN rises to get 'Counter-Attack' from the table.)*

OWEN. I've not changed much, either. I came because I want you to do something for me.

SASSOON. Oh ... I'm not—

OWEN. I've got your new book here. I want you to inscribe it for me.

SASSOON. That was ... It was the first time we met!

OWEN. Yes, it was.

SASSOON. But only one book, this time? Then, you had dozens of them

OWEN. More or less.

SASSOON. Mmm ... Not quite the hero I used to be...?

OWEN. Well, I bought three hundred copies, but I thought doing them all at once might tire you. I'll bring one a day for the next three hundred days — if I may.

SASSOON. Be quiet ... And give me your pen. *(SAS-SOON starts, laboriously, to write.)*

OWEN. Have you seen the reviews?

SASSOON. Robbie is bringing them. Are they bad?

OWEN. No. But you've astonished them.

SASSOON. Splendid!

OWEN. I thought that might please you.

SASSOON. They don't like being astonished, of course. Are they indignant as well?

OWEN. Some of them.

SASSOON. I got the book out just in time, then. I can't see that there'll be any more. Not from me. Not now ... Now, it's up to you. *(SASSOON hands back the book.)* Come on, tell me. What are you doing?

OWEN. Oh, that's not important. I don't want to talk about me. This — how did it happen?

SASSOON. Idiocy. Chiefly mine. Come on, tell me. I'm out of touch with everything.

OWEN. Well...

SASSOON. *(prompting him)* Robbie says you've met Osbert Sitwell...

OWEN. Yes, he introduced us.

SASSOON. And...?

OWEN. He's a bit alarming, isn't he?

SASSOON. Oh. And Edith?

OWEN. She's even more alarming.

SASSOON. So you didn't get on?

OWEN. Well, I think we did. Scott Moncrieff showed 'Mental Cases' to Edith — for their Anthology this year.

SASSOON. 'Mental Cases?'

OWEN. I'm sure I sent it to you. It's Craiglockhart, really.

SASSOON. Remind me—

OWEN.

"Who are these? Why sit they here in twilight?
Wherefore rock they, purgatorial ..."

SASSOON.

" — These are men whose minds the Dead have
    ravished.
Memory fingers in their hair of murders...
(He falters.)
Multitudinous murders they once witnessed — "
(SASSOON, as if attacked by remembered horror, involuntarily cries out. OWEN is very alarmed but tries to cover it.)

OWEN. Let me ... Can I get you something?

SASSOON. No. *No, no!* (OWEN grips his hand. SASSOON struggles to recover.) Thank you. So ... Scott Moncrieff ... he showed it to them, and ...? *Tell me!*

OWEN. Well, they want more.

SASSOON. They'll publish?

OWEN. Yes. If I'm too late now, they'll go in next year.

SASSOON. Well. Come on, tell me the rest.

OWEN. Er ... Robbie has been talking to Heinemann.

SASSOON. Yes? Well?

OWEN. I have to get my things typed and send them to Heinemann. Then he'll give them to Robbie — for *his* opinion.

SASSOON. And what is Robbie's opinion?

OWEN. Well, he ... Oh, you know.

SASSOON. So — Heinemann will publish?

OWEN. Robbie thinks he will. *(This is what SASSOON needed to recover.*

SASSOON. Oh ... I think I shall be very smug indeed. To have been proved totally right — no matter how slow I was to realize.

OWEN. Without you, none of it would have happened.

SASSOON. But of course it would. It would just have happened later, that's all. *(OWEN recognizes the signs of improvement.)*

OWEN. How are you feeling?

SASSOON. Rather like a cat who's fallen into the cream churn.

OWEN. *(grinning)* No, I mean — are you feeling all right?

SASSOON. I'm getting better by the minute.

OWEN. Are you up to helping me with this? *(He gets his notebook from the table.)* I've been jotting down ideas for a preface to the book.

SASSOON. It's got that far?

OWEN. Well — in case. May I?

SASSOON. I'm waiting!

OWEN.

"This book is not about heroes. English Poetry is not

yet fit to speak of them.

Nor is it about deeds, or lands, nor anything about glory, honour, might, majesty, dominion, or power, except War.

Above all I am not concerned with Poetry.

My subject is War, and the pity of War.

The Poetry is in the pity.

Yet these elegies are to this generation in no sense consolatory. They may be to the next. All a poet can do today is warn."

(OWEN looks for confirmation from SASSOON, who thinks about it.)

SASSOON. You need help? From me?

OWEN. Will it do, do you think?

SASSOON. I think it will do. Just as it is.

OWEN. Of course, there's no chance that it would come out before next year.

SASSOON. Have patience.

OWEN. I'll try. Oh, did you know the 'Nation' has published another one of mine, 'Futility?'

SASSOON. I don't remember that...

OWEN. No. It was while you were in France ... By the time my book's out, it will be too late — I hope. It should all be over. Don't you think so?

SASSOON. I can't see why it should ever stop. Do you know, I caught this *(his wound)* in the same square mile of France where I was shot last year?

OWEN. Will you tell me about it?

SASSOON. It wasn't much. *(OWEN comes to sit beside him. He is very earnest.)*

OWEN. I *do* want to know. Will you?

SASSOON. Why?

OWEN. In case I go back.

SASSOON. Tell me you're going back and I'll stick a bayonet through your leg. That should stop you.

OWEN. *(with a half smile)* I think you would, too.

SASSOON. You might have to live with a limp, but you'd *live*.

OWEN. Scott Moncrieff has talked about a job in the War Office in London.

SASSOON. Can he arrange that?

OWEN. But if I took it ... well, then I'd never know.

SASSOON. About yourself?

OWEN. Yes.

SASSOON. Are you still not sure?

OWEN. I shall never be sure unless I know what ... what happens. What it feels like when the bullet hits you. What you feel when you think you're dying. I've got to know that and face it — the worst I can imagine.

SASSOON. That's hard.

OWEN. Yes. But I can't go blindly, just because I'm ordered to go. I haven't got that sort of courage. My death has got to be my decision — my choice.

SASSOON. Then surely you're talking about *true* courage, aren't you?

OWEN. *Am* I? ... I'm certain I could never do what you've done — go out alone, at night, into No Man's Land, capture a trench, and then ... sit there writing poems. *(SASSOON grows angry, both at Graves and at the way OWEN is torturing himself.)*

SASSOON. You've been talking to Graves—

OWEN. He told me something about it. About when you—

SASSOON. Well, he's no right! ... Wilfred! All that's got nothing to do with courage. It's more like being drunk than being brave. Bravado, perhaps. Elation? Anger, certainly. All those things. I'm not proud of it.

OWEN. But you've never been proud of anything you've done, have you?

SASSOON. Yes, I think I have, sometimes. But not *this* ... It might have been a death wish ... All I'm certain of is that I had to do something. I was violently angry with the whole of the war. And it was my private revenge more than anything else ... *(SASSOON stops. He has said too much.*

OWEN. Revenge? *(SASSOON stares at him: the only way OWEN might be convinced is if he is told the whole story. SASSOON begins by sounding matter-of-fact, a manner which he finds difficult to sustain.*

SASSOON. When I first went out to France, I crossed the Channel with a young officer — David. He was 19. Came from Wales. Straight from school to Officer Training. He'd learned nothing. No ... More particularly, he'd not learned bitterness. He had all those things we should be born with: truth, integrity, gentleness, patience. He was cheerful as if it was always summer. His smile was ... One afternoon we borrowed a couple of horses and rode out to a village near Amiens, and had tea with so many cakes — a schoolboy would have been sick for a week. *(OWEN is completely still, afraid of what he may hear.)* He shouldn't have died, you see. He'd had no life. And he trusted us — the world. He trusted *me.* I should have died, not him. So, when he'd gone, I ... *(He looks at OWEN and has to stop.)*

OWEN. How did it happen?

SASSOON. He went up to the trenches without me. He went on a raid with a wiring party. He was shot in the throat and choked in his own blood ... We buried him on the slope of a hill — the words of the service were drowned out by mortar and machine-gun fire. We dropped him into a hole in the ground, wrapped in a sack ... *That's* all there was of him ... That's when I found out about death.

OWEN. You needed revenge?

SASSOON. I tried to die. I'd made up my mind to die. I did things I ... I can't believe, now. I'm sure I was mad ... And it doesn't go away. A few weeks ago, in France, there was a man with his jaw blown off by a bomb. His head was covered in bandages — face completely hidden — but ... the sound of his breathing ... And I thought, David died like *that*. Then — the same anger, the same madness.

OWEN. He's "Soldier David", isn't he? In "The Last Meeting" and "A Letter Home?"

SASSOON. They wouldn't let me have my revenge, you see. I was too great a risk. Quite right. They took me out of the Line. And so I wrote about him to — to keep him alive for a bit longer.

OWEN.
"...His name shall be
Wonder awaking in a summer dawn,
And youth that, dying, touched my lips to song."

SASSOON. Yes.

OWEN. I'm sorry. I shouldn't have made you remember.

SASSOON. But you do see, don't you? There's nothing in my sort of courage you could possibly want for yourself. You find *your* way. Not with anger, not for revenge — and *not* in *madness!* (*OWEN, somewhere between grief and anger, has a new strength.*)

OWEN. You're being very stupid! All you've told me about is caring and compassion — and love.

SASSOON. (*confused*) I'm ... I'm tired. I don't think I want to talk for a while.

OWEN. (*disappointed*) You want me to go ?

SASSOON. No! Please, not yet ... Your new poem — read that to me. (*OWEN opens his notebook, but after a couple of lines he addresses the poem to SASSOON.*)

OWEN.

"Move him into the sun—
Gently its touch awoke him once,
...In Wales...whispering of fields half-sown.
Always it woke him, even in France,
Until this morning and this snow.
If anything might rouse him now
The kind old sun will know.

Think how it wakes the seeds—
Woke once the clays of a cold star.
Are limbs, so dear achieved, are sides
Full-nerved, still warm, too hard to stir?
Was it for this the clay grew tall?
Oh, what made fatuous sunbeams toil
To break earth's sleep at all?"

(*OWEN'S response to the story of David Thomas is, for SAS-SOON, unpredictably generous, and he starts to see OWEN dif-*

ferently, with a sense of discovery. OWEN has reached a decision. His deference to SASSOON is now less, his affection more apparent.)

SASSOON. You, who 'write so big' — and *are* so big.

OWEN. It's not enough, Siegfried, is it?

SASSOON. It's what you do better than any of us ... *(And even that is not enough for OWEN. SASSOON looks around.)* It's a beautiful day out there in the garden. Why don't you move *me* into the sun?

OWEN. Is that allowed?

SASSOON. *I* will allow you.

OWEN. I knew it was a silly question.

(OWEN pushes him into the garden area upstage. Lights are reminiscent of the Milnathort sequence in Act One.)

SASSOON. Mmmm ... Reminds me of that line of yours, "Rich-odoured flowers so whelmed in fetid earth..."

OWEN. You used not to like that, as I remember.

SASSOON. I still don't. Luscious...

OWEN. It is, isn't it?

SASSOON. Ah! You know it yourself, now. Good. "Now my worldly task is done..."

OWEN. I knew it then. Too arrogant to admit it, that's all.

SASSOON. Never met anybody less arrogant in my life.

OWEN. That was only with you. It would have been more than my life was worth.

SASSOON. That's true ... You know, you're not nearly as timid as you used to be.

OWEN. Not with *you.*

SASSOON. Well — you used to think me very grand,

didn't you? "Stuck-up," you told me.

OWEN. Yes — but you were.

SASSOON. That is absolute rubbish!

OWEN. *(laughing)* That's *exactly* what I mean! But in those days I could see you only as someone with all the gifts I envied — and all the privileges I wanted for myself: your home, Marlborough, Cambridge...

SASSOON. Only for a year. Too bloody lazy to work for my degree.

OWEN. At least that was your decision. I couldn't even get the scholarship ... Why did you really go down from Cambridge?

SASSOON. I wasn't good enough. I didn't need a degree to tell me I had a third rate intellect — and absolutely no "Academic Bent" ... What an idiotic phrase that is!

OWEN. My teacher told my father he thought I had an academic bent. My father looked very worried. He thought it meant that with reading Keats all day, I was getting round-shouldered.

SASSOON. I do like the sound of your father. I think I'd find him very reassuring.

OWEN. I wonder. Do you know, when he heard I'd been passed fit for General Service, he wrote saying, 'Gratified to hear you're normal again.' *(They both enjoy that.)* You never knew your father, did you?

SASSOON. Not really. I was only five when he left my mother—nine when he died. But my mother—oh, she had ideas of her own. She thought me her 'second self', and she called me Siegfried because she had a fierce passion for Wagner...Thank God we never had a sister. Can you imagine—Brünnhilde Sassoon? *(The laughter grows.)*

OWEN. Is that true? The hero of 'The Ring?'

SASSOON. Have I never told you? Oh, yes. Heroism is a kind of social obligation on me — inflicted at the font. And look where it's got me now ...! *(OWEN takes the opportunity he has been waiting for. He is suddenly very serious, very intent.*

OWEN. It would help me if you could tell me about it. *(SASSOON realizes that he has trapped himself. He decides to make light of it.)*

SASSOON. Oh ... It was another piece of bravado! ... I'd been getting more and more tense ... jumpy — you know.

OWEN. Yes. And ...?

SASSOON. And then — I couldn't stand it any longer. I went across the Line with a corporal — Davis, first rate chap. We threw bombs at a machine-gun post — I'm sure we missed the thing — and then ran back. We stopped for a breather when we got near our own Line. I ... took off my tin hat—

OWEN. *What?!*

SASSOON. Well, it was hot out there. I ... stood up, and — well, we had a very keen sergeant in our Company, and he knew a German when he saw one. Next thing I knew, it felt as if I'd been hit by a sledge-hammer on the side of my skull.

OWEN. It was one of your *own* men?

SASSOON. Oh, yes. First rate shot, too. Glad he wasn't on form that day. If he'd hit half an inch to the left — well, you'd have been saying your Anthem over me ... I say, do you think he'd been bribed by the War Office? I'm sure they've been out to get me, ever since I was discharged from Dottyville. Nearly made it this time.

OWEN. Did you think you'd ... that you'd die?

SASSOON. Certain of it. And, do you know, I lay there — all this stuff oozing out of my head — thinking, 'my last words ought to be memorable.' Siegfried's final aria, and all that. But I couldn't think of a single thing to say except, 'My head hurts.'

OWEN. And that was it?

SASSOON. Yes! That's all there is. You're right: this war is *not* about *heroes*.

OWEN. It's really about boys of nineteen being shot in the throat and dying before they've had time to live — and to learn *why*. I think it's about the annihilation, the wanton destruction of everything we love. *(The reminder is a shock. SASSOON is tiring and barely audible.)*

SASSOON. "You have cried your cry; you have played your part."

OWEN. I didn't hear. What was that?

SASSOON. It was on the boat. I tried to write something. Still worrying about the last words, I suppose ... Wilfred, I'm suddenly feeling very tired. Do you think we could go in? *(OWEN wheels him back. When they are there:)*

OWEN. Tell me what you wrote.

SASSOON. It doesn't work, I can't do it. It starts—
"For the last time, I say war is not glorious,
Though lads march out superb and die victorious..."
(He stops. OWEN is very gentle.)

OWEN. It can't ever be said for the last time, though, can it? *(But SASSOON, exhausted, is at his lowest.)*

SASSOON. There's no help for it ... The last lines are, "Oh, my heart,

Be still; you have cried your cry, you have played
   your part."
*(OWEN sees his despair and goes to him. He takes SASSOON'S
hands in his.)*

SASSOON. All you have achieved, you pig-headed man, is
the wholly impossible. — And don't argue! I'm the best
judge of that. ... You must sleep, now.

SASSOON. Sleep, yes ... *(But he suddenly senses finality in the
hand clasp.)* I'll see you again? *(OWEN collects his things.)*

OWEN. Things to do. But I'll see you as soon as I
can.

SASSOON. Oh. Good.

OWEN. Until then...

SASSOON. Until then. *(OWEN makes sure he is sleeping
before he crosses to the other side of the stage. They are lit
separately.)*

OWEN. My dearest Mother, I can tell by so many signs
that Siegfried is really unnerved this time. Now I must
throw my little candle on his torch and go out again. I
think I am more glad than afraid. I shall be better able to
"Cry my cry, to play my part." The words belong to the
greatest friend I have. *(OWEN looks across at SASSOON.)*
My dearest Friend, Everything is clear now. I am in hasty
retreat towards the Front. *(SASSOON is trapped in the
wheel chair.)*

SASSOON. I'd no idea you'd already decided. If I'd
known—

OWEN. You'd have stabbed me through the leg ... If
you'd said through the heart or the brain, I'd have let you
do it.

SASSOON. Is it because of me, or ...? *Why?*

OWEN. My subject is war. I told you. What more is there to say that you will not better understand *un*said?

SASSOON. I didn't even try to stop him. If I'd *known*...

OWEN. We must all eat, drink and be merry, for tomorrow we — *live!* And the day after tomorrow, live, live, *live!* ... *(repressing an imminent panic:)* Lance Corporal Jones, my excellent batman, has been trying to cheer me up because he thought I was sad ... I suppose I have been thinking too wildly, and so crying a little. For only you to hear.

SASSOON. Wilfred? Was it my fault? *(OWEN seems to consider the question, then, without answering, collects his shoulder-pack, with a steel helmet attached to it.)*

OWEN. Dearest of Friends, Today is my last day in England, and serenity that Shelley never dreamed of crowns me. I wonder — will it last?

SASSOON.
"For now, he said, my spirit has more eyes
Than Heaven has stars; and they are lit by love..."

OWEN. Yes. I will remember him. In a village near Amiens, there is still a shop where you can get tea, and enough cakes to make a schoolboy sick for a week. I'll remember him for you when I go up to the Line. That will be any hour now.

(An explosion. OWEN puts on the helmet and moves upstage, where he stands in silhouette.)

SASSOON.
"He stood alone in some queer sunless place
Where Armageddon ends. Perhaps he longed
For days he might have lived; but his young face
Gazed forth untroubled ..."

(A louder explosion. SASSOON, still imprisoned in his chair, folds the red blanket on his lap.)

SASSOON. The news from the Front was changing. We began to advance, and the German troops began to lose their faith in ultimate victory. At the end of September, we started the Great Attack — and we passed the Hindenburg Line...

(Another explosion. OWEN moves downstage, takes off his helmet, and sits on a bench or chest — his dug-out area.)

OWEN. Very dear Siegfried, I have been in action for some days. Our experiences passed the limits of my abhorrence. I lost all my earthly faculties and fought like an angel. You'll guess what happened when I tell you that I am now commanding the Company — and that, in the Line, I had a seraphic boy-lance-corporal as my sergeant major. You'll remember I mentioned my excellent batman, Jones. In the first wave of the attack, he was shot in the head and thrown on top of me. He lay there, his blood soaking my shoulder, for half an hour. It's still there, crimson, on my tunic.
SASSOON.
"I saw his round mouth's crimson deepen as it fell,

Like a Sun, in his last deep hour;
Watched the magnificent recession of farewell,
    Clouding, half gleam, half glower,
And a last splendour burn the heavens of his cheek.
    And in his eyes
The cold stars lighting, very old and bleak,
    In different skies."

(A more distant explosion.)

OWEN. I can't say I suffered anything, having let my
brain grow dull. My nerves, then, are in perfect order. My
senses are charred. I shall feel again as soon as I dare, but
now I must not. I don't take the cigarette out of my
mouth when I write *Deceased* across their letters ...
Siegfried, I don't know what you'll think, but I've been
recommended for the M.C. — and I've recommended
every single N.C.O. who was with me. I'm glad of it — for
the confidence it will give me at home.

*(OWEN has taken out the Military Cross ribbon from his pocket
and pins it on while SASSOON speaks the official citation. Distant
gunfire is heard throughout.)*

SASSOON. "For conspicuous gallantry and devotion to
duty in the attack on the Fonsomme Line on 1st/2nd
October, 1918. On the Company Commander becom-
ing a casualty, he assumed command and showed fine
leadership and resisted a heavy counter-attack. He per-
sonally manipulated a captured enemy Machine Gun in
an isolated position, and inflicted considerable losses

on the enemy. Throughout, he behaved most gallant-
ly..." *(OWEN relaxes and leans back.)*

OWEN. I think, now, for me, it may all be over for a
long time. We are marching steadily *back*. What are you
doing? Can you tell me?

SASSOON. Very dear Wilfred, Doctor Rivers came to see
me. He tells me I shall never be passed fit to go back to
the Line. I wanted to go back — I *longed* to — as an Obser-
ver, an Official War Correspondent, to report the truth.
But when they asked what qualifications I could offer for
a job with the Ministry of Information, I said the only
qualification I could think of was that I'd been shot in the
head. *(OWEN grins, widely.)* Then, Eddie Marsh arranged
a meeting with his chief, Winston Churchill. As you
know, since Gallipoli he's had to make do with the Ministry of Munitions. Well, he seemed to think some of my
poems were "memorable" and — oh, he was really very
friendly. But then the Politician took over and he began
to make a fine speech about all the benefits brought to
mankind by warfare. For example, the general improvement in sanitation. "War," he said, "is the normal
occupation of man." War ... "And gardening." I think he
was serious. Eddie started to look very worried. Admiral
Fisher was waiting outside while all this was going on!
Oh, Wilfred, I shouldn't be here with these people! Waking and sleeping, I dream of you out there and I'm filled
with longing to be with all of you again ... Don't throw
away *your* medal. When you come back, you can flaunt it
in the face of that unspeakable Colonel who doubted
you. *(OWEN leans forward, suddenly urgent.)*

OWEN. Dearest Friend, We're getting rumours about

some sort of Armistice! The old soldiers go on cleaning their rifles, unbelieving. But do you know what's happening?

SASSOON. On the fourth of October, the German Commander in Chief formally asked for an Armistice! But the Kaiser dismissed him. Then, the German people began a revolution—

OWEN. We've heard their navy's mutinied — their army's deserting in regiments! *Is it true?*

SASSOON. It was all true. At last, incredibly, we could see an end of it. When Austria surrendered, we knew it could only be a matter of days. It was the third of November ... *(SASSOON has risen. He pushes his chair away, out of the action, and stands listening to OWEN intently, hoping for a reprieve.)*

OWEN. Dearest Mother, I'm writing in a smoky cellar. The smoke is so thick, I can hardly see. And so thick are the inmates that I can hardly write for nudges and jolts. It's a great life ... There is no danger down here. Or if there is, it will be over before you read these lines. I hope you are as warm as I am — as serene in your room as I am here. Of this I am certain: you could not be visited by a band of friends half so fine as those who surround me. *(SASSOON moves to his desk.)* Dearest Friend, Some poems to tempt you to a letter. And I'll give you my mother's address. I know you would try to see her if — if I fail to see her again.

(An explosion. SASSOON looks at a sheet of OWEN'S paper but the words are for himself.)

SASSOON.

"I would have poured my spirit without stint
But not through wounds; not on the cess of war.
Foreheads of men have bled where no wounds were..."
(OWEN rises and steps towards him, directly addressing him.
SASSOON turns, appalled, to see him, and hears as an
accusation:)

OWEN.

"...I am the enemy you killed, my friend.
I knew you in this dark: for so you frowned
Yesterday through me as you jabbed and killed.
I parried; but my hands were loath and cold.
Let us sleep, now..."
(OWEN lies down, knees drawn up, an arm across his face, keep-
ing out the light. SASSOON'S fear sounds harsh.)

SASSOON.

Why do you lie with your legs ungainly huddled,
And one arm bent across your sullen, cold,
Exhausted face? It hurts my heart to watch you.
(OWEN stirs in his sleep. SASSOON, with relief, picks up the red
blanket and moves to the dug-out space.)
Drowsy, you mumble and sigh and turn your head...
You are too young to fall asleep for ever;
And when you sleep you remind me of the dead.
(SASSOON, with great care, places the red blanket over him.
Kneeling above him, he watches him sleeping.) At 5:45 on the
morning of the fourth of November, his Company led
the crossing of the Sambre Canal. His men remember
him, going among them, encouraging them, joking with
them. He began to help them to fix some duckboards at
the edge of the water. That's where he was machine-

gunned to death. *(OWEN turns over and is completely covered by the red blanket, like a pall. SASSOON watches him, then stands.)* The Armistice was signed exactly one week later, on the eleventh of November, at five o'clock in the morning. At eleven o'clock, the fighting stopped. At twelve o'clock, the victory bells were ringing out in Shrewsbury. Bands were playing, crowds cheering. His mother and father began, in gratitude, to pray. Then the telegram arrived. *(He feels cold. He puts on his jacket and stands above his desk.)* I was staying near Oxford when I heard the bells. My mind was empty. Except for the belief that no amount of bell-ringing or drunken crowds waving flags should dull the memory of what that war had been. Or make us forget how much we had to mourn! *(His anger dies. He explains:)* Of course, I've never been able to accept his loss. Too much of myself went with him. All these years afterwards — there's still a chasm in my private existence which, briefly, he had filled. I think that's why I remember. *(He looks at the papers on which he has been working. He tears them across. He has a new resolution.)* I want to remember the delight he often brought me; to believe that with me he was at his best; to recall no shadow of unhappiness or of misunderstanding between us. About him, too, I say that,

"...When I find new loveliness to praise,
And things long-known shine out in sudden grace,
Then will I think: 'He moves before me now.'
So he will never come but in delight,
And, as it was in life, his name shall be
Wonder awakening in a summer dawn,
And youth that, dying, touched my lips to song."

(For the moment, he has been comforted. He remains still.)

(Lights fade to blackout.)

THE END OF THE PLAY.

NOTES ON THE SOURCES

ABBREVIATIONS

SIEGFRIED SASSOON

SS: Poems   War Poems of Siegfried Sassoon, ed Rupert Hart-Davis, (Faber & Faber, 1983)

Journey   Siegfried's Journey, (Faber, 1945)

Sherston 1   Memoirs of a Fox-hunting Man, (Faber, 1928)

Sherston 2   Memoirs of an Infantry Officer, (Faber, 1930)

Sherston 3   Sherston's Progress, (Faber, 1936)

WILFRED OWEN

WO: Poems   The Poems of Wilfred Owen, ed. Jon Stallworthy, (Hogarth Press, 1985) — with references to the Complete Poems and Fragments, 1983.

Letters   Collected Letters, ed. Harold Owen and John Bell, (Oxford University Press, 1967). In the Selected Letters, pub. 1986, the letters are numbered in accordance with the Collected edition.

* * * * *

ACT ONE

pp. 9-15   For Sassoon's description of this occasion, see Journey, ch. 6, pp. 64-5.

pp. 11 & 14   Quotations from Aylmer Strong, A Human Voice, (Elkin Mathews, 1917). Sassoon misquotes 'Th' epopt..' in Journey p. 65.

p. 16	'And one whose spear...' Shelley, *The Revolt of Islam,* Canto V.
	'Strange Friend, I said...', *WO: Poems,* p. 125, 'Strange Meeting'. The poem was almost certainly begun after Owen had left Craiglockhart, although the seeds of it may be seen in fragments of work he had begun there. Certainly, the influence of Sassoon's 'Enemies' and 'The Rear Guard' can be noticed. I have placed this extract here as a familiar landmark, indicating the stature of Owen's mature work.
p. 17	'the Hell in which we met...': for Sassoon's description of Craiglockhart, cf *Sherston 3,* part one, where it is called 'Slateford'.
pp. 17 - 20	'My darling Mother...', etc.: extracts from *Letters* 528, 532, 540.
p. 18	'Sing me at morn...': this version is from Dominic Hibberd's ed. *War Poems and Others,* 'Song of Songs', p. 72.
p. 19	Sassoon's statement of protest pub. variously, inc. the *Times,* 31 July 1917, and *Sherston 2,* part ten, V.
p. 20ff.	For Sassoon's recollection of this meeting, cf *Journey,* ch. 6. Also *Letters,* 540-46 & 565.
p. 22	'He is made one with nature...', Shelley, *Adonais,* XLII.
	'He was beside me now...', *SS: Poems,* p. 31, 'The Last Meeting'.
p. 24	'War is our scourge...', *SS: Poems,* p. 15, 'Absolution'.

p. 25	'To my Brother', *SS: Poems,* p. 18.
p. 26	'The Bishop tells us...' *SS: Poems,* p. 57, 'They'.
p. 27	'I told you, I wrote to her...': some of the images are drawn from *Letters,* 481-2, and from 'Exposure', *WO: Poems,* p. 162.
p. 28	'He drowsed and was aware...', *SS: Poems,* p. 52, 'The Death Bed.'
p. 31	'H.G. Wells...', cf *Letters,* 541. The scene is suggested by *Letters* 541-7 and *Journey,* ch. 6
	The Dead Beat': the version of 22 August 1917, in Dominic Hibberd, op. cit., p. 73. See also *Letters,* 485-6.
p. 32	'Rich-odoured flowers...', from a poem of 1912, 'Deep under Turfy grass', *WO: Poems,* p. 39. *Journey,* ch. 6, suggests that Sassoon found 'She dreams of golden gardens and sweet glooms' too "luscious", but this line appears in 'The Kind Ghosts', which was written on 30 July 1918. (*WO: Poems,* p. 158.)
	'To Eros', *WO: Poems,* p. 92. The poem seems to refer to Owen's reasons for leaving Dunsden Vicarage in 1912.
p. 33	'Sweat your guts out...', *Letters,* 541
	'Out there we've walked...': *WO: Poems,* p. 142, 'The Next War'.
p. 34	'Exposure', *WO: Poems,* p. 162. Opinions vary about when the poem was begun, starting with Edmund Blunden's reasonable claim that Owen's dating of Feb. 1916 must have been a slip of the pen for

Feb. *1917,* since it clearly relates to his experiences in France at that time. Jon Stallworthy equally reasonably claims that a longer period of gestation would be required and suggests it should be Feb. *1918.* Sassoon believed that Owen worked on it at Craiglockhart: "I see in it that W. had been influenced by Barbusse's *Le Feu* — the English translation of which I made known to him in Aug. 1917." In *Journey,* he says that Owen withheld the poem from him. He explained later that he had never contested the earlier dating, "...being dated previous to W. knowing me, provides proof that he was working on his own creative line before that (my influence on him having been exaggerated)."

<table>
<tr><td>p. 35</td><td>'These last days...', Letters, 546, 548 & 555.</td></tr>
<tr><td></td><td>'I have an uncomfortable suspicion...' cf Journey ch. 6 and the note on 'Exposure', above.</td></tr>
<tr><td></td><td>'As a rule, he was reticent...', suggested by the manuscript notes for Journey, ch. 6.</td></tr>
<tr><td>pp. 36-37</td><td>'Dreamers' and 'The Rear Guard' were both published in 'The Hydra'.</td></tr>
<tr><td>p. 37</td><td>'On Saturday, I met Robert Graves...', Letters, 551.</td></tr>
<tr><td>p. 38</td><td>'Do you know, Owen...' Letters, Appendix C.</td></tr>
<tr><td>p. 40</td><td>'Robert always was a bit dogmatic...' For the origin of this anecdote, cf Sherston 2, part six, 1, where Graves appears as David Cromlech.</td></tr>
</table>

p. 42   The Milnathort scene is suggested by *Letters*, 555, and *Journey*, ch. 6. pp. 63-4 & 59-60.

For Owen's experiences at Savy Wood, see *Letters* 505, 506, 508, 510.

p. 43   'There are ways of getting round it...' *Letters*, 547.

'I can't shout any kind of protest...' cf Harold Owen, *Journey from Obscurity III*, pp. 162ff.

pp. 46-48   The amendments to 'Anthem for Doomed Youth', inc. Sassoon's suggestions, can be seen in Dominic Hibberd, op. cit., pp. 145ff, and are reproduced in C.D. Lewis' 1963 edition of the Poems and in Jon Stallworthy, *Wilfred Owen* (1974) as well as his *Complete Poems & Fragments*.

p. 49   'Grame...' *Letters*, 557; a note says "SS cannot explain this word". The couplet occurs on p. 17 of 'A Human Voice'.

pp. 50-51   'My dear Sassoon...' extracted from *Letters*, 557.

ACT TWO

p. 53   'You smug-faced crowds...' from *SS: Poems*, p. 119, 'Suicide in the Trenches'

'Jesus, make it stop...' cf *Letters*, 660, note.

'When I'm asleep...', *SS: Poems*, p. 94, 'Sick Leave'.

p. 54   'I sit alone...', cf *Letters*, 565, also Keats: 'Ode on a Grecian Urn', V.

'Their wrongs are mine...': paraphrase of *SS: Poems*, p. 108, 'Banishment'.

'Robbie took me to the Reform...': the London sequence is suggested by *Letters, 565, 559, 584, 585*. Some details are drawn from Robert Graves' description of his own wedding in 'Goodbye to All That'.

p. 55   'Dr Rivers tells me...': the extent of Sassoon's problems in making his decision to go back to active service are described in *Sherston 3,* esp. part one, V., which also describes his dreams and discusses the nature of shell-shock.

'It is almost midnight...' *Letters, 578 & 571.*

p. 56   'He writes like a condemned man...': *Letters, 571.)*

p. 57   'I took the long road...' cf *Sherston 3,* part three.

pp. 58ff   The last meeting took place between 12th and 16th August, 1918. Owen had failed his Medical Board on 11th: in a letter to Scott Moncrieff (pub. in the 'Nation', March 1921) he said "I couldn't work it this time." He managed to get another Board on 26th, i.e. after the meeting with Sassoon, and was passed fit for General Service Overseas. cf *Letters* 640-644 and *Journey,* ch. 7.

Sassoon's *Counter-Attack,* pub. 27th June, 1918.

p. 61   'Mental Cases, *WO: Poems* p. 146. It was published in the Sitwells' anthology, *Wheels,* in 1919, along with 6 other poems by WO. The volume was dedicated to his memory.

'Robbie has been talking to Heinemann...':
cf *Letters,* 620.

p. 62   'This book is not about heroes...', from WO's notes for a Preface, pub. variously inc. *WO: Poems* p. 192, where the manuscript is reproduced as a frontispiece.

p. 64   'I shall never be sure...': cf reminiscences of Frank Nicholson in Edmund Blunden's *Memoir;* also *Letters,* 288.

'But I can't go blindly...': cf conversations recalled by Harold Owen in *Journey from Obscurity III.*

pp. 65-66   Sassoon's grief and anger at the death of David Thomas are vividly recorded in *Sherston 1,* part nine, IVff, (where he is called Dick Tiltwood); as well as in 'The Last Meeting' and 'A Letter Home'. He was killed on 18th March, 1916. The *Diary* for 1916 records the event and Sassoon's reaction.

p. 66   'His name shall be...': *SS: Poems,* p. 31, 'The Last Meeting', III, written in memory of David Thomas; see also p. 22 above, and pp. 72 & 79 below.

p. 67   'Move him into the sun...': *WO: Poems,* p. 135, 'Futility'. Line 3: 'In Wales' and 'half-sown' appear in earlier drafts.

pp. 69-70   Sassoon's memories of childhood, Cambridge, etc., are recorded in *The Old Century* (1938) and *The Weald of Youth* (1942). There are also references in Felicitas Corrigan, *Siegfried Sassoon: A Poet's Pilgrimage* (1973).

p. 78	'I would have poured my spirit': *WO: Poems,* p. 125, 'Strange Meeting'; see the note re p. 16 above.
	'Why do you lie...': *SS: Poems,* p. 129, 'The Dug-Out'.
	'His men remember him...', cf Blunden's *Memoir,* and Lt. J. Foulkes' description of Owen's death.
p. 79	'I was staying near Oxford...': cf *Journey,* chs. 10, 6 & 7.
	'a chasm in my private existence...' *Journey,* ch. 7.
	'When I find...': 'The Last Meeting': see notes on pp. 22, 65, 66, & 72 above.

* * * * * * *

ACKNOWLEDGEMENTS

Quotations from *The War Poems of Siegfried Sassoon* (Faber & Faber, London, 1983) by permission of George Sassoon;

from *Siegfried's Journey* (Faber, 1945) by permission of the publisher;

from *Wilfred Owen: Collected Letters,* ed. Harold Owen & John Bell, (Oxford University Press, 1967) by permission of the publisher;

from Wilfred Owen, *Collected Poems* (Chatto & Windus, London, 1963) by permission of the publisher.

FURNITURE & PROPERTY PLOT

FURNITURE (see A Note on the Setting, p. 6)
D.R. Small writing table and chair (OWEN)
R. of C. : two small arm chairs and wine table
U.S.R. : oak chest
L. of C. : large writing table and swivel chair (SASSOON)
U.S.L. of SASSOON's table : hat stand
D.L. : small table and chair

PROPERTIES
D.R. table:
    Blank manuscript paper
    blue letter paper
    pens and pencils
    poems on loose sheets inside the covers of an old
      exercise-book (p. 30)
    cutting from The Times (p. 19)
    2 sets of proofs of the *Hydra* (pp. 36 & 37)
    letter from Robert Graves (p. 37)
    OWEN's pocket-notebook (pp. 46 & 66)
    5 copies of *The Old Huntsman* (p. 20)

    ACT II
    add: *Counter-Attack* (p. 58)

R. of C. wine table:
    empty bottle of Burgundy and 2 stem-glasses

    ACT II
    strike bottle and glasses

L. of C. table:
    Blank manuscript paper
    manuscript sheets (the OWEN memoir)
    4 War diaries
    SASSOON poems in folder (*Dreamers* etc. p. 36)
    cutting from The Times (p. 19) and other cuttings
    H.G. Wells letter in dim pink ink (p. 31)
    pens & pencils in tankard
    photographs, ash tray, general dressing
    in table-drawer: faded copy of note & *Strange Meeting*
        (p. 16)
    letters from OWEN to his mother & to SASSOON

    ACT II
    add; tumbler with whisky

U.S.R. chest:
    ACT II add: shoulder pack with steel helmet and re-
        volver (p. 73)

U.S.L. hatstand:
    SASSOON's woollen bath robe
    trench coat
    Army cap (Royal Welch Fusiliers)
    golf bag with wooden clubs and cleaning rag.

D.L. OFF STAGE:
    ACT I: one-pint tankards
    ACT II: wheel chair, in it a blood red hospital
        blanket

PERSONAL:
    SASSOON: brown sealed envelope, watch, handker-

chief, *A Human Voice* (p. 9)
OWEN: carrying cap, gloves, cane, small shoulder-pack; in pockets: 2 sheets blue writing paper (p. 14), ms sheet of *Exposure* (p. 34), list of names (p. 24)
ACT II: Military Cross ribbon and pin (p. 75)

COSTUME PLOT

SASSOON:
Brown Norfolk jacket, tweed trousers, beige shirt, green tie, brown shoes. *On hatstand:* woollen bath robe, trench coat, Army cap (Royal Welch Fusiliers).

OWEN:
Uniform of a Second Lieutenant in the Second Manchester Regiment, 1917-1918: tunic, breeches, puttees, boots, cap, gloves, cane, 'Sam Browne' belt and shoulder strap, watch.

STAGE PLAN
NOT ABOUT HEROES

OWEN

CHEST

SASSOON

HAT STAND

EXTERIOR

CLOTH LIFTED TO FORM SKY-CLOTH

REMEMBERING MR. MAUGHAM
Garson Kanin

Memoir / 2m

Remembering Mr. Maugham is an intimate glimpse into the life of W. Somerset Maugham – one of the most brilliant, prolific and secretive writers of the 20th century. This graceful two-character, one-act play adapted by Garson Kanin from his memoir is a treasure trove of private conversations, amusing anecdotes and candid recollections of his beloved friend and confidant. Through decades of friendship, Kanin and Maugham poignantly reminisce about life, art and the unconquerable human spirit.

FLAGS
Jane Martin

Drama / 6m, 2f, extras / Unit Set

This fierce new drama by the author of Talking With , Anton in Show Business and Keely and Du redefines patriotism as it brings the tragic fallout from the war in Iraq home to America's heartland. When a grieving father inverts our nation's most revered symbol, the family is swept into the vortex of a chaotic war machine. Portrayed in the press as both 'heroes with a cause' and 'enemies of the state,' they become embedded in a bitter struggle for their very survival. Jane Martin gives voice to the white-hot rage and sorrow of our time, delivering a shock-and-awe display of theatrical force.

"...a powerful gut-punch of a play, blisteringly contemporary."
- Minneapolis Pioneer Press

"Powerfully mines heartbreak, loss, and disillusion to universalize the Iraq war. Brave, deeply compassionate, and, most importantly, very good drama."
- Minneapolis City Pages

SKIN DEEP
Jon Lonoff

Comedy / 2m, 2f / Interior Unit Set

In *Skin Deep*, a large, lovable, lonely-heart, named Maureen Mulligan, gives romance one last shot on a blind-date with sweet awkward Joseph Spinelli; she's learned to pepper her speech with jokes to hide insecurities about her weight and appearance, while he's almost dangerously forthright, saying everything that comes to his mind. They both know they're perfect for each other, and in time they come to admit it.

They were set up on the date by Maureen's sister Sheila and her husband Squire, who are having problems of their own: Sheila undergoes a non-stop series of cosmetic surgeries to hang onto the attractive and much-desired Squire, who may or may not have long ago held designs on Maureen, who introduced him to Sheila. With Maureen particularly vulnerable to both hurting and being hurt, the time is ripe for all these unspoken issues to bubble to the surface.

"Warm-hearted comedy … the laughter was literally show-stopping. A winning play, with enough good-humored laughs and sentiment to keep you smiling from beginning to end."
- TalkinBroadway.com

"It's a little Paddy Chayefsky, a lot Neil Simon and a quick-witted, intelligent voyage into the not-so-tranquil seas of middle-aged love and dating. The dialogue is crackling and hilarious; the plot simple but well-turned; the characters endearing and quirky; and lurking beneath the merriment is so much heartache that you'll stand up and cheer when the unlikely couple makes it to the inevitable final clinch."
- NYTheatreWorld.Com

CPSIA information can be obtained at www.ICGtesting.com
Printed in the USA
LVOW12s1439210514

386773LV00017B/706/P

9 780573 640445